GEOGRAPHY OF SOCIO-ECONOMIC DISPARITIES IN JHARKHAND

GEOGRAPHY OF SOCIO-ECONOMIC DISPARITIES IN JHARKHAND

Syed Naushad Ahmad

AUTHORSPRESS

Worldwide Circulation through Authorspress Global Network
First Published 2004
by Authorspress

E-35/103, Jawahar Park
Laxmi Nagar, Delhi-110 092

e-mail: authorspress@yahoo.com

Typeset in NewCenturySchlbk by Chitra Computers

Geography of Socio-economic Disparities in Jharkhand
ISBN 81-7273-177-9

Printed in India at Tarun Offset, Delhi.

Foreword

Regional imbalance and poverty are closely interconnected. States or regions in India which have favourable environment, and have given attention to the application of technology in agriculture as well as in industries are economically far ahead compared to other regions or states. Even if the environment is harsh, man's dynamism, education and application of technology and innovative skill can save the situation. If initiatives are taken in keeping with the environment, the development will be sustainable.

The present work relates to social and economic disparities in the Jharkhand portion of Chotanagpur plateau. The southeastern part is well developed and has important industrial complex. Sindri, Jharia, Bokaro, Jamshedpur and Ranchi which have important industrial complex while the remaining parts of the plateau are under developed.

Dr. Naushad Ahmad in this book has made cogent suggestions as to how the conditions of the tribal in the north-eastern parts can be improved, which industries should be promoted to increase the purchasing power of the people and the regional imbalance can be reduced.

The book is full of facts, supported by statistical techniques and observation of the author. It should interests all those who are interested in the tribal life, regional planning and alleviation of poverty. The book deserves a copy on the shelf.

Padma Shri Prof. M. Shafi
Former Vice President of International Geographical Union (IGU)

Preface

Despite a growing concern of the Planning Commission to reduce regional disparities in social services and economic infrastructure between backward and developed areas, this objective to a greater extent has not been achieved due to the fact that identification of backward areas are still lacking at the micro and meso levels. It was argued that in view of wide regional disparities in the levels of development a common strategy of development will not be sufficient for all regions, and each region must have its own strategy of development which is suitable for its requirements. Such regional approach is only possible and successful, if backward regions and their typology are identified at the micro, meso and macro levels in terms of a large number of socio-economic indicators of development.

The present book is an outcome of my research work in which a modest attempt has been made to identify the backward regions of Chotanagpur Plateau (Jharkhand) at the sub-division level which may provide a base and guidelines to the planners and policy makers to bridge the gap between developed and backward regions of this state.

This book is spread over seven chapters. The first chapter examines the statement of the problem, concept of disparities, database and data constraints and review of literature. The second chapter gives a detailed account of the geographical outline and resource endowments of the study area. Chapter three deals with selection and significance of indicators for measurement of regional disparities. Chapters four and five have been devoted to delineate regional patterns of disparities in terms of 20 indicators covering a wide area such as health facilities, housing and environment, educational development, urbanisation, security, occupational status, size of land holdings, levels of agricultural development, levels of industrial development as well as overall socio-economic development. Chapter six explains the dimensions of disparities and their underlying causes. Chapter seven highlights regional patterns of inequalities between tribal and non-tribal population in Chotanagpur Plateau as tribals constitute an important segment of the total population of the area, and they are extremely backward in almost every walk of life compared to their non-tribal counterpart which is a matter of great concern.

I wish to express my deep sense of gratitude to my supervisor, Dr. Amar Singh Ex Head of the Deptt. of Geography, D.S, College, Aligarh, for his invaluable guidance and advice on various aspects of this study. I am also equally thankful to Professor Mehdi Raza, Deptt.of Geography, A.M.U., Aligarh, for his discussion and suggestions at different stages.

I am also indebted to Professor Mohammed Shafi, Deptt, of Geography, A.M.U., Aligarh, who in spite of his busy schedule has been benevolent enough to provide me time for his critical suggestions.

I record my gratitude to Dr. Feroz Ahmad Khan, Jamia Millia Islamia, New Delhi, and Dr. Abdul Munir, A.M.U., Aligarh, for their help in solving some of the methodological problems during my research.

The list of acknowledgement would be incomplete without due thanks to my research colleagues, Mr. Zeya Ashfaqullah, Dr. Zulfiquar Ali Khan, Dr.Md. Nazim, Dr.Md. Shamim, Dr. Ibal Imam, and Dr.Farooque Azam.

Lastly I am very thankful to Mr. Munne Khan for his cartographic help.

S. Naushad Ahmad

List of Figures

List of Tables

Contents

1

Introduction

STATEMENT OF THE PROBLEM

One of the serious problems which India is facing today is the problem of regional disparities. It results in social, economic and political instability. The current tension and strain in the Indian polity are essentially a function of inadequacy of the strategies evolved since independence to correct inequalities and distortions embodied in the Indian space economy during the period of colonial rule.[1] These stresses in recent years have acquired alarming proportions and have been weakening the foundation of Indian unity and integrity. The recent development in the north-east states which are extremely backward are pointers to such danger. The growing trends of regionalism, secessionism and separatism in these areas stem from frustation of the people, particularly the young generation, arising out of prolonged regional disparities. It has been observed that problems arising out of socio-economic disparities often get linked with linguistic and cultural affinities of the region. These problems take serious shape and subsequently become hard to eliminate.

Regional disparities and lopsided growth are also not conducive to economic stability and may well results in under-utilisation or even non-utilisation of natural and human resources, and in that process individuals are discriminated.

The problem of regional disparity is persistent all over India but is more acute in Chotanagpur plateau (Jharkhand). Though it is very rich in mineral resources, yet there is considerable spatial disparity in the level of development. Development interms of industrialisation, urbanisation, communication and other sectors are concentrated in few pockets which are largely confined in the south-eastern part, the rest of the region is extremely backward. The Chotanagpur plateau not only experiences regional disparity in socio-economic development but also there is marked inequalities in the level of living between the tribal and the non-tribal population.

The tribals form an important segment of demographic structure of the Chotanagpur plateau. They account for 30.25 per cent of the total population of the region. The socio-economic condition of the tribals of this region is very miserable. There is marked disparity in the socio-economic standards of tribals living in their areas of concentration as compared to the people of the surrounding areas. The reasons behind their abject poverty and inequality, are exploitation by non-tribal landlords, traders, contractors and bureaucrats as well as illiteracy, ignorance and conservatism of the tribals themselves. This cross-social and economic inequality has led to the volcanic outburst of the Jharkhand movement. In this context the present study assumes immense significance for diagnosing the problems and suggesting strategies for future development.

Regional disparities in socio-economic conditions are primarily the result of lack of uniform development of institutional and technological parameters that are needed to achieve transformation of society for the better. Thus the social reality is the reflection of operation of institutional and technological factors at different levels. Specially, the spread and assimilation of better technologies plays an important role as in course of time it can significantly modify and upgrade the socio-cultural milieu. But in reality in the present context technological development remains generally limited to a few developed regions, leaving other regions underdeveloped. The latter usually have to do with traditional technologies and are thus unable to satisfactorily satisfy the needs of the growing population. Thus the spatial patterns of disparities between developed and underdeveloped regions continue to persist relatively even though in absolute terms considerable development may have taken place in the underdeveloped region. We may, therefore, state that the socio-economic development of the developed regions is often at the cost of increasing underdevelopment of other regions.

In order to understand the processes involved in creating disparities between developed and underdeveloped regions it is necessary to keep in mind that inequality is an outcome as well as manifestation of factors which are predominantly structural and are deeply rooted in social, economic, cultural, historical and political mesh of the area. The manifestations however have spatial ramifications which become inequalities when viewed in the perspective of social norms and general pattern of living. The task of social geographers is mainly to decipher spatial variations, but in the process the threads of structural variations should be also picked up.

There are various ways of analysing spatial disparities in the level of socio-economic development, but the regional approach which permits the vertical integrations of socio-economic conditions and horizontal variations over space is most important, Using the spatial approach a unit of spatial organisation of society in terms of certain selected indicators of the level of socio-economic development can be identified.

Once the regions of underdevelopment have been identified and delineated and the main factors contributing to disparities in the level of development analysed, strategies for a more just spatial order may be suggested.

AIMS AND OBJECTIVES

The main objectives of the present study are as follows:

1. To identify the regions of different levels of development in terms of a large number of social and economic indicators sectorwise as well as in aggregate.

2. To study dimensions of disparities.
3. To highlight factors and processes responsible for emerging patterns of socio-economic disparities.
4. To measure cross-inequalities between tribals and non-tribals.
5. To suggest remedial measures for its minimisation.

CONCEPT OF DISPARITY

One should not be confused with the terms 'disparity', 'diversity' and 'inequality'. All three terms seem to be synonymous but they have different meanings. Disparity refers to differences in socio-economic development. It arises as a result of the failure to exploit development potentials of a region hidden in its initial resource endowments in comparison to other regions. It is, therefore, caused by factors which are not natural or physiographic but human, institutional and historical and/or economic technological. It is the creation of man's developments efforts. Hence, it may be called developmental inequality.

On the other hand the term 'diversity' denotes differences in the initial resource endowments largely of natural or physiographic character leading to territorial specialisation and division of labour through exploitation of resource advantages, comparative as well as absolute.

Inequality connotes differences in socio-economic organisation, including political groups, classes or economic sectors and institutions. It is caused by differences in social, ethnic, cultural and economic parameters and differences in opportunity structures and access to development benefits that arise because of exploitation of man over his brethren. Thus disparity is present in horizontal direction whereas inequality is present both in horizontal as well as in vertical direction. The term spatial inequality is more comprehensive which includes both static and dynamic elements. Within the rubric of spatial inequality all three kinds of inequalities are contained. Thus spatial inequality means the study of uneven development in space characterised by certain patterns of association of different variables (including space, environmental and socio-economic variables) in an area contributing to the syndrome of inequality.

DATABASE AND DATA CONSTRAINTS

The study is based on secondary sources of data collected from census publications and different departments concerned. The disparities have been perceived in terms of a wide range of indicators covering the areas of health, housing, environment, education, security, urbanisation, occupational structure, status of scheduled tribes and general population, size of land holding, agricultural and industrial development, etc. The spatial dimensions of disparities have been measured using the technique of standardised 'Score Additive Model' and 'Factor Analysis'. Subdivisions have been chosen as units of analysis keeping in view the availability of data and nature of the problem.

In a backward state like Jharkhand the availability of data on each and every aspect of society is too difficult. Even whatever data are available are often not uptodate, complete and regular in the requisite form. Although an attempt has been made to make the nature of analysis as comprehensive as possible, yet there have been certain limitations, e.g., the data of per capita income, expenditure and the size of land holding belonging to different categories of population are not available. If such types of data were available the study would have given a more comprehensive picture of inequality.

Initially the aim was to conduct a similar study for 1991, and to compute the coefficient of congruence between the two decades, but paucity of data prevented a complete comparable study.

Generally, concept and definitions of variables change from time to time which compound the problem of comparison at different points of time for showing trends of any attributes.

Also rural-urban or male-female data on all variables are not available. Therefore it is very difficult to study disparities between rural and urban areas as well as between males and females.

The frequency of publication is not regular. Most of the data which should have been published on an annual basis come after the lapse of two or three years. Similar is also the case with census data. Though census operation is held after an interval of every 10 years, its information is published too late. Owing to this limitation portrayal of the current situation is very difficult. It has also been observed that some of the variables which were published in previous issues are not found in later ones.

REVIEW OF LITERATURE

Works on regional disparities have evoked a considerable interest, particularly after the realisation of the influence of regional factors in development. This is borne out by the large number of studies carried out in this field. Attempts at the national level have been replicated at the state and lower levels. There is also a shift from the overall development to sectoral and micro-sectoral studies. While there are welcome signs, there are certain areas which still remain unexplored. Though there are a number of studies pertaining to regional disparities at the national, state or even smaller areal unit, yet it is lacking in the state of Jharkhand. Earlier attempts to measure regional disparities emphasized on the final outcome, and per capita income was used as the sole indicator of the level of development, and it was then perceived in terms of economic growth. Later on however, development was treated as a broad-based concept that incorporated changes in other spheres of human life. This necessiated the use of a large number of indicators related to different facets while determining relative development.

Sen Gupta and Sadasyuk (1961) have worked out the economic regionalisation of India in an attempt to provide an hierarchy of regions useful in national planning.[2]

Schwartzberg (1962) attempted to regionalise the socio-economic development of India. The use of a composite index of development brought out areal differences in the levels of development, although these differences could not be further put to rigorous regional analysis as the data were on the basis of states (prior to 1956), which are not ideally suited to reveal regional differences.[3]

The National Council of Applied Economic Research (NCAER) has arrived at the district level per capita income and the proportion of 'income' of each district according to primary, secondary and tertiary activities. These data, though crude, serve to relate the income pattern with land use structure and occupational patterns and urban-industrial development in broad regional analysis.[4]

The map prepared by Bhat (1964) indicates the pattern of industrial development in the background of resource potential in different areas. Contiguous areas of urban-industrial development occurring along the edge of the Krishna-Godavari Delta or from the Coimbatore plateau to the Kerala coast are the resultants of a relatively developed agricultural-based industries. The patterns of levels of development as brought out by mapping the index values seem to explain the causes of disparities in the levels of development in an objective way.

The study shows that areas having low levels of development coincided roughly with those having low land productivity or lack of good resource base and occurrence of small and stagnant towns without much industrial activity and inter-town relationship. On the other hand, Hyderabad occurs as an 'island' of development in the relatively underdeveloped area of Telengana.[5]

Pal (1965) made a more systematic attempt in the construction of a composite index of selected variables which permit several stages of analysis in relation to the group of variables contributing to overall development; with a study of the all India level it may be regarded essentially as a contribution to methodology in areal differentiation by factor analysis. To be of use in policy decisions these studies need to incorporate some of the important factors like per capita income and production which are directly related to the levels of development.[6]

Mitra (1965), using a somewhat different method, has grouped 324 districts of India into four levels of development. For his study he selected 63 variables and these were grouped into six convenient blocks. The variables pertain to natural factors, agricultural, infrastructure, traditional economy, human resources, organised industry, etc. This study is unique for its simplicity and systematic approach. Nevertheless, the author himself pointed out in his introductory remarks that the lack of more important indices and methods of giving weights to different variables is a limitation to this study. The data in per capita income is difficult to calculate below the state level.[7]

Nath (1970), on the basis of state and district level data, worked out the regional patterns of economic development and economic growth within India. An analysis of the level of economic development has been made for both states and districts, but an analysis of growth rates has been made only for states. The level of economic development of states has been measured in two ways: (i) on the basis of per capita income, and (ii) through the use of a composite index of economic development based on four indicators. An analysis of economic growth has been made with the help of data on growth rates of population, agricultural output, per capita value added in industry, and per capita income. He mapped the states of India into two categories of relatively developed and less developed.[8]

Nair (1971) examined the empirical validity of the hypothesis that as the income of a nation increases the inter-regional differences in income between the regions of the nation automatically diminish. He used three measures in his analysis: the quotient of disparity, the weighted coefficient and the income relatives. He reached the conclusion that a reduction in inter-regional income differentials does not necessarily follow automatically from an increase in the income of the nations.[9]

Varma (1972), using per capita product as an indicator of development, analysed time series of regional disparity in per capita product during the period 1949-50 to 1967-68 in Pakistan. He used fitted equation in his analysis.[10]

Sharma and Katiyar (1972) emphasized the need of developing a synthetic index of development rather than a single index of a specific variable because it does not give an overall picture. They developed certain indices and used the composite index method to determine the level of development of Uttar Pradesh.[11]

Nair (1977), using rank correlation technique, studied regional disparities/in industrial wages in India. His study reveals that wages in organised industrial sector have been very low in the states of Jammu and Kashmir and Andhra Pradesh while the reverse is the case with Bihar and Maharashtra. The states of Karnataka, Orissa and Madhya Pradesh seem to be improving their position in this regard with the opposite being the situation in Assam and Punjab. But the relative position of the states does not seem to undergo major changes during the period while there are some signs of decline in disparities.[12]

Sampth (1977), using measure similar to the coefficient variation, studied inter-state inequality in income during 1951-71. He measured inequalities at three levels; at the level of regional net domestic income, at the level of sectoral income and the level of regional per capita income. He prepared the index of economic performance in order to show the relative positions of the states.[13]

Prakash (1977) assessed the regional inequalities and economic development in relation to infrastructural facilities in India. He selected several infrastructural factors, the various population characteristics that reflect the development of infrastructure: the determinants of industrialisation, the development of power, irrigation and agricultural implements, and road transportation, communication and banking services. He obtained two important conclusions from the analysis of development of individual regions in various fields: (i) There is no region which is equally developed or underdeveloped in all the fields. For example, developed areas like Tamil Nadu, West Bengal, Andhra Pradesh, Maharashtra, Kerala and Punjab are underdeveloped in one or more of the fields like literacy, workforce participation rates, per capita power consumption, irrigation or mechanisation of agriculture while the underdeveloped regions like Jammu and Kashmir, Nagaland, Arunachal Pradesh, Mizoram, Rajasthan, Bihar and Madhya Pradesh are quite developed in one or more fields like literacy, density of population, workforce participation rates, urbanisation, power consumption and road transportation. It would, therefore, be more useful for policy purpose to identify individual areas of deficiency rather than to bracket regions as developed or underdeveloped in general so that the remedial measures to make up the deficiencies could be evolved and implemented; (ii) The other important result is that the same regions/regions come under the category of developed regions if one indicator is used while they fall in the category of underdeveloped regions if some other indicator relating to the same field is used for classification. It implies that an appropriate indicator should be chosen to determine the stage of development of the regions.[14]

Prakash and Rajan (1979), using the Gini coefficient, measured the degree of concentration of agricultural inputs and agricultural development. They reached the conclusion that agricultural productivity per hectare is widely diffused but agricultural inputs like iron plough, tractors, fertilisers, high yielding variety (HYV) seeds, irrigation, etc., are highly concentrated. There are hardly any regions which are not totally under-developed or developed.[15]

Ajit (1979) analysed the trends in inter-regional and inter-districts income differentials in Uttar Pradesh over the period 1951-71. His study revealed that per capita income of western Uttar Pradesh is higher than eastern.[16]

Bronger (1986) measured levels of development in terms of 36 indicators in Andhra Pradesh taking districts as a unit of the study. He applied factor analysis in identifying backward and developed regions as well as investigating dimensions and dynamics of development in the state.[17]

Dadibhavi (1989) measured regional disparities in terms of net domestic product at factor cost at three points of time: 1960-61, 1970-71 and 1975-76 in Karnataka he took district as a unit of analysis. His study reveals that there is a wide variation in the level of development during 1960-61 and 1975-76. Inequality reduced marginally but ranking of the districts remains the same. Variations in active participation and the degree of industrialisation have increased but there has been a decline in respect of effective work participation rate, labour productivity, degree of organisation, literacy rate, and composite index of infrastructure, indicates that effective participation and productivity are the only significant variables to inter-districts variation in Karnataka.[18]

These studies of regional patterns of developments in India provide a conceptual and methodological framework to extend them to the micro-level with necessary modifications. The present study employs extensively concepts and methodology developed in these studies to analyse the patterns of regional development in the area of study.

REFERENCES

1. Raza, M., "India: Diversities and Disparities", in Singh, H., *Planning Regional Development and Disparities in India*, Criterian Publication, New Delhi, 1989, p. 20.
2. Sen Gupta, P. and Sadasyuk, G., Economic Regionalisation of India: Problems and Approaches, in A. Mitra(ed.) *Census*, Vol. 1, No. 8, New Delhi, 1961.
3. Schwartzberg, J.E., "Three Approaches to the Mapping of Economic Development in India", *Annals of the Association of America Geographers*, Vol. 52, 1962, pp. 455-468.

4. National Council of Applied Economic Research, The District Income Differentials 1955-56, *Occasional Paper*, No.6, New Delhi, 1963.
5. Planning Commission, Government of India, *Resource Development Regions and Divisions of India*, New Delhi, 1964.
6. Pal, M.N., "Regional Disparities in the Level of Development in India", *Fifth Econometric Conference*, New Delhi, 1965.
7. Mitra, A., Levels of Regional Development in India, *Census of India*, 1961, Vol. I, Part I-A (i), 1965.
8. Nath, V., "Levels of Economic Development and Rates of Economic Growth in India — A Regional Analysis", *The National Geographical Journal of India*, Vol. 15, Part 3-4, 1970, pp. 183-198.
9. Nair, K.R.G., "Inter-state Income Disparities in India", *India Journal Regional Science*, Vo1.3, No.2, 1971, pp. 46-56.
10. Varma, P.C., "Regional Disparity in per capita product in Pakistan", *Indian Journal of Regional Science*, Vol.4, No.1, 1972, pp. 90-98.
11. Sharma, P.N. and Katiyar P.C., "Identifying Under Developed Districts of Uttar Pradesḥ", *Indian Journal of Regional Science*, Vo1.6, No.1, 1974, pp. 30-38.
12. Nair, K.R.G., "Regional Disparities in Industrial Wages", *Indian Journal of Regional Science*, 1977, pp. 207-215.
13. Sampath, R.K., "Inter-State Inequalities in Income in India 1951-71", *Indian Journal of Regional Science*, Vol.9, No,1, 1977, pp. 1-12.
14. Prakash, S., "Regional Inequalities, and Economic Development with Special Reference to Infrastructural Facilities in India", *Indian Journal of Regional Science*, Vo1.9, No.2, 1977, pp. 172-195.
15. Prakash, S. and Rajan, P., "Regional Inequalities in Madhya Pradesh", *Indian Journal of Regional Science*, Vol.II, No.l, 1979, pp. 1-12.
16. Singh, A.K., "Regional Inequalities in a Backward Economy: A Study of Trends in Inter-Regional and Inter-District Income Disparities in Uttar Pradesh", *Indian Journal of Regional Science*, Vo1.2, 1979, pp. 36-47.
17. Bronger, D., "Regional Disparities as a problem of spatial Development Planning in Countries of Third World Case of India with Reference to Andhra Pradesh", *Annals of the National Association of Geographers India*, Vol.6, No.1.
18. Dadibhavi, R.V., Regional Disparities in Karnataka in Singh, H. (ed.), *Planning Regional Development and Disparities in India*, Criterion Publication, New Delhi, 1989.

2

The Study Area: Its Environmental Setting

DELINEATION OF THE REGION AND ITS ADJUSTMENT WITH ADMINISTRATIVE BOUNDARIES

The Chotanagpur plateau lies between 21°58 N and 25°18 N latitudes and 83°22'E and 87°57' longitudes. It is bordered by Uttar Pradesh and Chhattisgarh in the west, West Bengal in the east, Orissa in the south and Bihar in the north. It covers approximately an area of about 79,476^2 kilometres. It is roughly triangular in shape. Its maximum length in the east-west direction is about 457 kilometres and width in the north-south direction is about 310 kilometres.

The Chotanagpur plateau lies dominantly in Jharkhand including small portions of West Bengal and Madhya Pradesh. However, the present study is concerned with only that portion which lies in Kharkhand. The study area includes the districts of Santhal Pargana, Dhanbad, Hazaribagh, Giridih Palamau, Ranchi and Singhbhum. However, this region has been re-organised into 18 districts recently.

GEOLOGIC AND GEOMORPHIC CHARACTERISTICS

The Chotanagpur plateau remained unaffected by any uplift since Cambrian or Vindhyan times up to the Tertiary era. During this long period of quiescence, it was subjected to large-scale denudation which turned it into a low lying peneplain. As a side effect of violent Himalayan movement the Chotanagpur plateau uplifted in tertiary times. This earth movement changed the previous landscape of the Chotanagpur region into a new one. At present it is not entirely a peneplain but consists of a series of plateaus separated by steep scarps on which rivers descend. These rivers, instead of flowing through broad channels, occupy relatively deep-cut meandering channels.[1]

The surface rocks of a larger part of the Chotanagpur plateau belong to the Archean system which is considered to be the oldest in age. These rocks include (i) Lava and basic intrusive igneous rocks (ii) Granite and gneiss and (iii) Schist and iron-ore series belonging to Dharwar. Dharwar lies over lavas and basic rocks. It was first formed by sedimentary rocks and has been metamorphosed and crystallised to the extent that it is difficult to distinguish it from their basement Archeans. This area is very rich in iron ore, maganese ore and cyanite and extends over a large area of Singhbhum and Hazaribagh, especially in Kodarma. They form isolated hills and ranges of Khargpur and Rajgir. The mass of granite rocks which extends throughout the plateau of Chotanagpur is known as Chotanagpur granite-gneiss. It is associated with the veins of Pegmatite. All granite rocks of the region are not of the same age, for instance, the granite rocks of Singhbhum which contain copper deposits are of much later date than the greater part of Chotanagpur granite-gneiss. The next in geological formation are the Kolhan series consisting of horizontally bedded lime-stones, shales and conglomorates and largely found in south Singhbhum district. The next in age are the Vindhyan rocks which are composed of limestones and sandstones. They are found in the extreme north-west of Palamau district. Then comes the Gondwana rocks which contain the largest deposit of coal in India. They are found in sandstone beds of Damodar and Auranga river valleys. In the eastern part of Santhal Pargana, Rajmahal traps of Jurassic period overlie the Gondwana rocks where dykes of dolerite have penetrated in the coalfields. The hills lying in the western part of Ranchi and south Palamau are capped by the outliers of Deccan trap of cretaceous period. They have now been mostly changed into laterite which at some places form an important source of bauxite.

The Chotanagpur plateau is a region of great physical diversities and has resulted from various processes operating through geologic times. It consists of a large number of plateaus and hills, each occurring at a height different from others. Most of the plateau region has an elevation exceeding 305 metres with a greater part rising about 610 metres above sea level. The heart of the plateau is constituted by Hazaribagh and Ranchi plateau which are separated by the Damodar basin. The Pat areas of these two plateaus has maximum height ranging from 762 to 915 metres. Parasnath is the highest hill (1,350 m) situated in the eastern part of Hazaribagh plateau. On the basis of elevations, morphologic features and-imminent slopes the plateau of Chotanagpur may be divided into the following physical units:

1. North Koel basin
2. Pats
3. Ranchi plateau
4. Hazaribagh plateau
5. Lower Hazaribagh plateau
6. Rajmahal highlands
7. Adjoining Ganga plain
8. Damodar basin
9. Panch Pargana plains
10. Porhat Dalma highlands
11. Dalbhum plains.
12. Dhanjori range
13. Kolhan uplands
14. Singhbhum plains
15. Simdega plateau

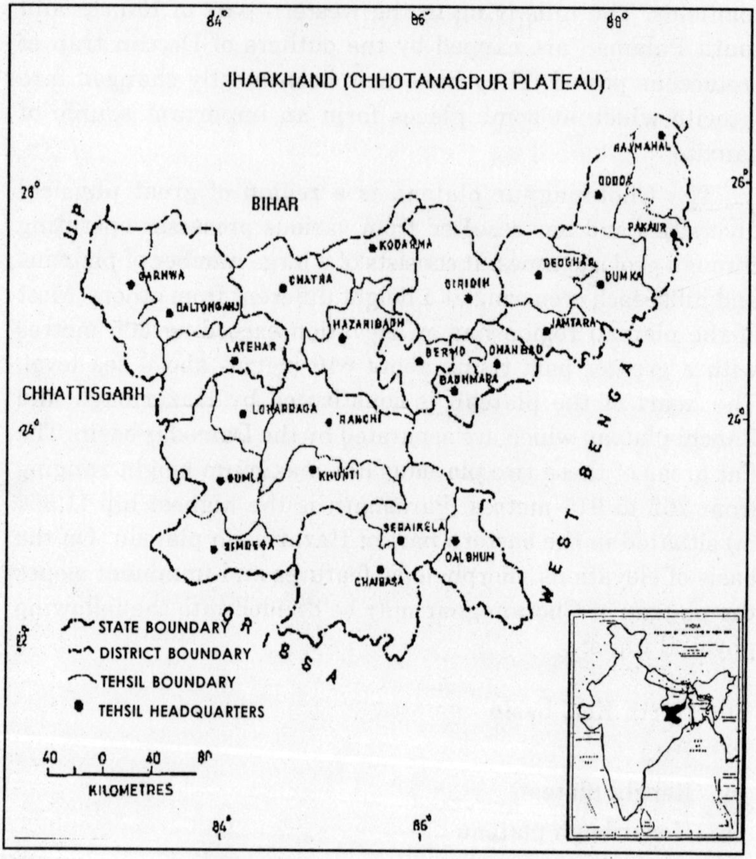

Figure 1: Administrative Divisions

1. *North Koel Basin*: This is the westernmost part of the Chotanagpur plateau which covers a large part of the Palamau and Garhwa districts. The surface of this region is extremely rugged and the landscape presents an intricate, confused pattern consisting of narrow valleys that alternate with spurs and ridges of various shapes and sizes.[2] Few small patches of levelled land which are surrounded by hills may also be observed in this region. This region has an average elevation of 360 metres above

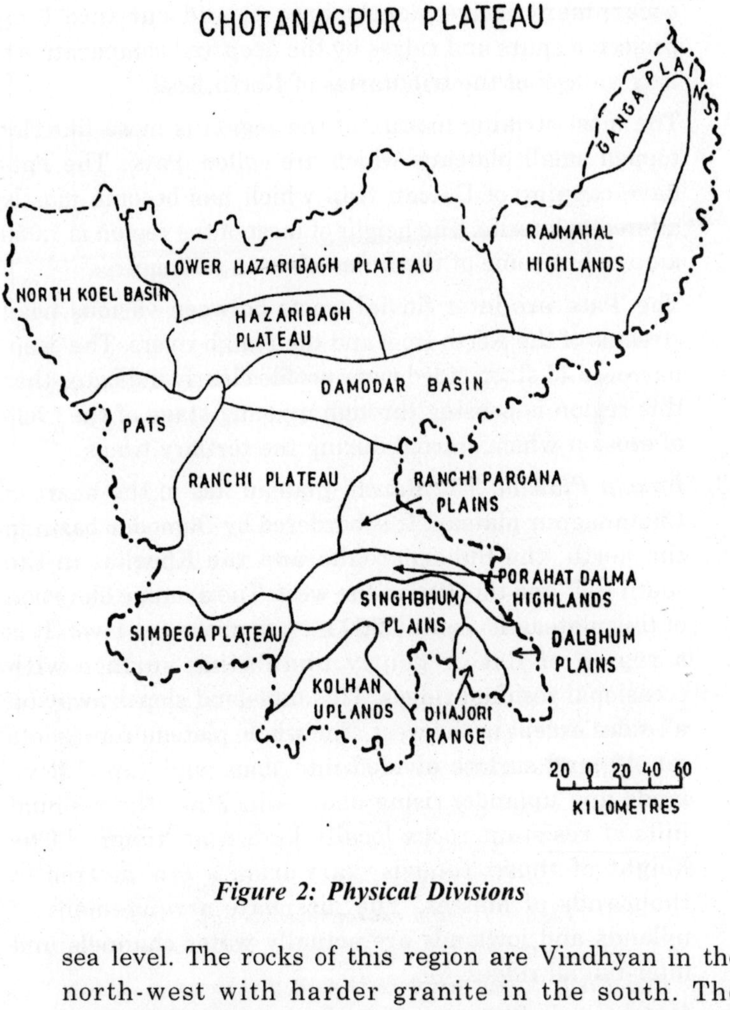

Figure 2: Physical Divisions

sea level. The rocks of this region are Vindhyan in the north-west with harder granite in the south. The important rivers are the Son, the north Koel, the Amnat, the Gogra and the Kankar. All of them except the Son rise from neighbouring highlands.

2. *The Pat:* The Pat tableland lies west of the Ranchi plateau. It is triangular in shape with its base in the north and its apex in the south. It is enclosed by escarpments from north and east. The eastern escarpment is unbroken and extends from Chandwa to Palkot. The northern

escarpment is frequently broken and cut into long projected spurs and ridges by the deep and comparatively long valleys of the tributaries of North Koel.

The most striking feature of the region is mesa-like flat topped small plateaus which are called 'Pats'. The Pats have capping of Deccan trap which has become mostly altered to laterite. The height of most of the region is 1,050 metres but some of them rise above 1,150 metres.

The 'Pats' are inter fluvial tracts between various head streams of the North Koel and the Sankh rivers. The deep, narrow and steep-sided river profile clearly indicates that this region is passing through a young stage of the cycle of erosion which started during the tertiary times.

3. *Ranchi Plateau*: The Ranchi plateau lies in the heart of Chotanagpur plateau. It is bordered by Damodar basin in the north, the Subarnarekha and the Kharkai in the south-east and the 'Pat' in the west. The average elevation of this plateau is about 6,000 metres above sea level. It is a region of flat or gently undulating surface with occasional residual ridges. This tableland slopes away on all sides except in the west. The whole plateau represents an old land surface divided into 'dons' and 'tanrs' (low-lands and uplands) rising above which are the residual hills of resistant rocks locally known as 'tongri'.[3] The height of these 'tongris' vary from a few metres to thousands of metres. The alternate arrangement of uplands and lowlands are actually water channels and inter-fluvial ridges.

4. *Hazaribagh Plateau* : The Hazaribagh plateau is the northern part of the central plateau which is separated from the main plateau by the Damodar trough. It is connected with the Ranchi plateau from the west by the broad ridge that forms the Auranga-Damodar divide. The Hazaribagh plateau is not a continuous surface but divided into three separate blocks arranged in an east-west elongation. The average elevation of Hazaribagh

plateau is about 600 metres. Its topographical features are more or less the same as the Ranchi plateau. But it is more dissected by deep gullies that extend from the river bed up to the centre of the plateau.

5. *Lower Hazaribagh Plateau* : The lower Hazaribagh plateau has an average elevation of about 380 metres. This plateau is characterised by an undulating surface with relict hills. Its eastern part is lower and gentler as compared to its western part. The northern part is marked by rocky hills and steep-sided valleys through which Sankari and its tributaries flow. The Braker river passes through the eastern portion of this region creating several basins. The Usari and Mohani are other important streams.
6. *Rajmahal Highland* : The Rajmahal highland comprises the north-eastern part of Chotanagpur plateau. It is enclosed by the alluvial tract of the Ganga from all sides except the south and west. It has resulted from volcanic eruption and has varied and picturesque landscape. It consists of several flat-topped plateaus and conical hills with an average elevation of 200 metres but some of them have elevation more than 450 metres. The whole hilly tract is made of bedded basaltic trap of post-Gondwana origin. The trap rocks are dark dolerite while the inter-trappeans beds. Consists of white and grey shales, carbonaceous shales, white and grey sandstone and hard quartzite.[4] The weathering of volcanic rocks has led to the formation of laterites which cap the higher flat-topped hills. The important rivers of this region are the Chitra, the Guman, the Mor and the Ajoy.
7. *Adjoining Ganga Plains* : The Ganga plains lie in the extreme north-west fringe of Santhal Pargana district between the river Ganga and Rajmahal hills. It covers an area of about 800 square kilometres. The alluvial tract that girdles the Rajmahal hills has greater elevation and steeper slopes than the adjoining Ganga plains, and transition is marked by a line of break-point in gradient.

8. *Damodar Basin :* The Damodar basin is located in the south-eastern part of the Chotanagpur plateau comprising the whole of Dhanbad, Hazaribagh and Giridih districts and part of Ranchi and Palamalu districts. This region has varied relief features comprising flat valleys, isolated hills, scarp fringes and miniature plateaus.[5] The elevation of this basin varies from 300 metres to 600 metres and the general slope is from east to west with an average gradient of 3°. The predominant rocks in this regions are shales, sandstone and granite inter-bedded with carbonaceous strata. The northern part of the basin is broken and rugged while the southern part is relatively plain containing some of the best rice lands.
9. *Panch Pargana Plain:* The Panch Pargana plain comprises a small tract in the south-eastern portion of Ranchi district. It is bordered by West Bengal in the north-east and Ranchi plateau and Dalma range in the west and south respectively. This plain has an average elevation of about 250 metres above sea level. The slope is gentle and the topography is the same, except along the rivers that have cut deep valleys and flow through incised meanders. The western part of this region is rugged. Various waterfalls are conspicuous features of this area, the Honshu being most important of them.
10. *Porhat Dalma Range:* The Porhat Dalma range lies roughly along the border of Singhbbum and Ranchi in the east-west direction. It was made of volcanic lavas. The backbone of Dalma range is formed by a great thickness of very resistant old lavas which were less affected by denudation and at present are in the form of residual ridges.[6] The continuity of this range is broken at Chakaulia where it looks very beautiful. The southern slope of this range is slightly steeper than the northern side affecting the agricultural resources and settlement.
11. *Dalbhum Plain:* The Dalbhum plain comprises the extreme south-eastern part of Chotanagpur plateau in

Singhbhum district. It extends over an area of about 800 square kilometres. This plain is an eastward extension of the undulating plain of Singhbhum. In fact, it is an erosional plain and has acquired its present form by denudation of anticline. This plain slopes to the east and south-east and its surface is undulating. It is drained by the Subarnarekha river and its tributaries.[7]

12. *Dhanjori Range:* The Dhanjori range occupies a small tract in the south-eastern portion of Singhbhum district. It is bordered by Dalbhum plain in the north-east and Singhbhum plain in the west. It consists of a group of small hills broken by streams. This region represents a variety of landscapes formed by rocks of varying resistance, hardness and altitude. The south-eastern part of this range extends up to Subarnarekha basin. The general elevation of this region is about 300 metres with several important hills among which are Charai Pahar, Mankarora, and Dalma Pahar. Dalma Pahar attains the highest elevation in the central tract. Some parts of this upland is covered with laterite and bear evidence of tertiary deposition and subsequent uplift.

13. *Kolhan Upland:* The Kolhan upland tract lies between the Singhbhum plain in the north and the state boundary in the south and east. Owing to have been made us of varying resistance it has varied relief features. It consists of sedimentary rocks such as sandstone, conglomorate, shale and limestone grouped under the name of Kolhan series. The Kolhan rocks are softer than rocks of iron-ore series, therefore have been eroded to a greater extent.[8] The elevation of this plateau varies from 450 metres to 300 metres above sea level. The surface, on the whole, is undulating, and it slopes downs on all sides. This plateau contains the source of several streams in its central part from where they radiate in different directions.

14. *Singhbhum Plain:* The Singhbhum plain lies in the central part of Singhbhum district extending over an area of about

2,000 square kilometres. It has an average elevation of 120 metres above sea level. The plain has been formed indifferently over softer mica-schist and shales as well as granite of Singhbhum and Chakardharpur.[9] Owing to a less diverse slope the entire region is cultivated and densely populated. This plain is drained by the Sanjai river, a tributary of Kharkai.

15. *Simdega Plateau:* The Simdega plateau occupies the south-western part of Ranchi district, It is bounded by Ranchi plateau in the north, the Porhat Dalma range, the Singhbhum plain and the Kolhan upland in the east and the state boundary in the south-west. This plateau is also rugged and hilly with turbulent streams, steep slopes, high cliffs and narrow valleys. It is drained by the South Koel and the Deo Nadi whose tributaries spread over the entire region. This region is still under forest cover but at some places fertile valleys occur.

HYDROLOGIC FEATURES

Availability and utilisation of water depends on the structure and physiography of the area. Therefore, it is essential that an appraisal should be made for the source of water.

The most important source of water is river. The Damodar, the Subarnarekha, the North Koel, the South Koel and the Sankh are the important rivers of Chotanagpur plateau. The Damodar is the most important river so far as the catchment area is concerned. It drains along with its tributaries an area of 11,078 square kilometres of Palamau, Hazaribagh and Dhanbad districts, which is 27 per cent of the Chotanagpur area. The annual rainfall in this basin is 55" whereas the total annual run-off comes to 53.10 lakh acre feet. The highest flood discharge recorded at Tenughat dam site is of the order of 250,000 cusecs[10] but in dry weather the discharge figure comes down to a few hundred cusecs. In the upper Damodar basin topography is undulating and forested. The Middle basin has coalfields of Ramgarh, Karnpura, and Bokaro and has industries.

Out of a total potentiality of 53.10 lakh acre feet, only 10 per cent has been harnessed and utilised. This area receives a fairly high average annual rainfall which is 1364.2 mm or 54". About 90 per cent of the total annual rainfall is confined to the four months from June to September.

The quantity of utilised water is 5.25 lakh acre feet; 1.25 lakh acre feet is used for agriculture and 4 lakh acre feet is consumed by domestic and industrial sector. It means that there is 47.85 lakh acre feet of water which is going waste. The Subarnarekha is the second most important river of this region. Its catchment area extends over 7,350 square kilometres of the total area of Chotanagpur. It serves the industrial centres of Ranchi, Muri Jamshedpur and Ghatshila. This basin receives a normal rainfall of 53" and has a total run-off of 54.28 lakh acre feet. In this basin, 29 per cent of the run-off is being utilised. Out of 12.98 lakh acre feet of harnessed water, 2.76 lakh acre feet goes to industries and domestic purposes and 12.98 lakh acre feet irrigates the crops. Untapped water is about 36.54 lakh acre feet. The South Koel river basin covers an area of 6,880 square kilometres. This region receives 58" of average rainfall. The total annual run-off in this basin is 50.28 lakh acre feet of which only 14 per cent has been brought under use. Consumption of water by agriculture and industries is 0.18 lakh acre feet and 0.52 lakh acre feet respectively. The quantity still awaiting exploitation is 49.58 lakh acre.

The North Koel river covers an area of 5,600 square km and receives a normal rainfall of 53". It has a total run-off of 23.50 lakh acre feet. So far only 1.986 lakh acre feet has been tapped for irrigation which is only 8.4 per cent of the available quantity. It means that about 22.50 lakh acre feet of water is to meet the future demand.

The upper Sankh basin has a catchment area of 3,187 square kilometres. The annual rainfall is 62" and the total run off is 19.75 lakh acre feet. As yet no attempt has been made by government to make use of this water.

So far no device has been sought to measure the exact quantity of sub-soil or underground water. But anyhow work in this field is being carried out by the "Ground water exploration project". Drilling operations in the mica field of Hazaribagh have found the existence of sufficient quantity of underground water in this area. Empirical works have shown that 30 per cent of the total rainfall percolates and forms the underground water. Thus the study area has 337,500 acre feet of underground water. The utilisation of sub-soil water depends on economic drilling which is truly speaking a function of structure and water table. In the study area the gneissic and granitic base makes drilling operation expensive. Added to it, the average depth of water level in this area is 30 ft to 35 ft as compared to only 6 ft in the plain areas. Besides, even if the underground water is tapped an open well has an irrigating capacity of only 3 acres against 6 acres in plain. Keeping an eye on the level of water which fluctuates with the amount of rainfall and temperature, the forested and undulating topography, and drilling cost, it can be safely inferred that only 9 per cent of the total underground water can be tapped economically.

There are numerous irrigation schemes. However, so far only 12 per cent of the total run-off has been collected in reservoirs for irrigation, drinking and industrial purposes. Schemes have been undertaken to utilise 2.2 per cent of the potential surface water which will irrigate 26 thousand acres of land. This surface water is also used for generation of hydel power. So far power produced from this source is of the order of 104 MW. Gealsud dam which is supposed to generate 60 MW is under construction; other schemes have been proposed with a total installed capacity of 1,017 MW.

There is enough potential water resource in this area which can be tapped for future development of the area. During the monsoon period rivers are in spate. This water can be supplied to large distances economically Hence it is desirable that industries should be located near abundant sources of river basins. Moreover, where industries exist, the level of water exploitation should be increased so that the water supply could be in pace with the increasing demand of the growing population and industries of that area.

CLIMATIC ATTRIBUTES

"Chotanagpur plateau experiences the characteristic monsoon climate having a seasonal rhythm running through all elements of weather."[11] Owing to tropical and sub-tropical location Chotanagpur comes under the south-west monsoon in the month of June, July and August. Due to its altitude (higher than 50°C) the temperature is moderate and somewhat uniform. The highest temperature recorded in May is 50ºC and the coolest month is December (25°C). The mean range of temperature is 32.2ºC in the west and 27.4°C in the eastern and north-eastern part of the region.

The climate of Chotanagpur plateau may be divided into three broad seasons:(i) winter season, (ii) summer season, and (iii) rainy season.

i) *Winter Season:* The cold weather season begins in November and lasts till the end of February. During this season Chotanagpur comes under the influence of high pressure developed over the north-western part of India, therefore it experiences anticyclonic conditions. The wind belows from the north-west to the south-east but the actual direction is controlled by relief. Temperature varies from 16°C to 7°C. The main characteristics of this season is clear and fine weather with pure air and azure blue sky. The days are slightly warm and sunny and the nights are cold. Little rainfall occurs by occasional invasion of western disturbance.

ii) *Summer Season:* From the first week of March to May Chotanagpur enjoys summer season. In May, the temperature rises sharply and the monthly mean temperature in this month reaches up to 29°C-32°C. On account of the high temperature low, pressure develops in the north-eastern part of the plateau. As a result the wind blows from the west with increasing velocity from 3.6 to 14.4 kilometres per hour. By the end of May the low pressure gets intensified and extends toward the west. The characteristic feature of this season, however, is the afternoon or evening storms which burst after the heat of the day and form the main source of the rain.[12] Dust storms, thunderstorms and whirlwinds are also experienced in this season. Winds remain normally very hot.

iii) *Rainy Season:* Mid June to mid-September is the season of rains with 90 per cent of total annual rainfall. The outburst of monsoon reduces temperature by 5°C slowly till September. High relative humidity and occurance of heavy rainfall are the main features of this season.

Chotanagpur as a whole receives 1,362.2 mm of average rainfall. The uneven distribution of rainfall is determined by undulating topography. It varies from 1,030.7 mm. to 1,817 cm. Areas laying above 900 metres have the maximum rainfall. In the north-west and north-east of the 'Pat' region the amount of rainfall decreases.

On account of the distance from the Bay of Bengal and rain shadow position of 'Pat' region, in the northern-fringe of Palamau, rainfall is less than 1164.2 mm. It is the district which suffers from the most severe drought in the Plateau where agriculture mostly depends on irrigation. Agriculture in this region is dependent on monsoon. The trend of rainfall is such that out of every five years normally two or three years produce a favourable monsoon. It is not uncommon to find that the crucial rain in September-October period (Hathia), which is essential for ripening paddy fields making crops prospects precarious.[13]

SOILS

The Chotanagpur plateau is largely covered by red soils but loose sandy soils are found in the Damodar basin, high level lateritic soils over the Pat region and regur and lateritic soils over lava surface of Rajmahal hills. The soils of Chotanagpur contains a high percentage of ferric oxide and bauxite which impart red colour to them. The granitic and gneissic rocks have given birth to deep red or even black soils which have sufficient content of potash and lime but nitrogen, phosphoric acid and humus contents are inadequate. The red soils are generally thin, sandy or gravelly on the uplands but thick and loamy in valleys and depressions. The regur of Rajmahal hills has originated from basaltic rocks and contains silicious matter, kaolin and potash. It also contains iron oxides and magnesia. The moisture retentive capacity of regur is very high and it is very fertile.

The soils of valleys have surpassed the upland soil in respect of fertility, moisture and clay content and have been brought under rice cultivation, whereas the soils of scrap and foothills area is infertile and consists of rock debris. Low water table and poor fertility is the characteristic of the area. Gully erosin is severe in this area. Wrong methods of ploughing the slopes, lack of deep-rooted vegetative cover and heavy showers of rains during monsoon are the chief causes[14] of this erosion.

SPATIAL DISTRIBUTION OF POPULATION

According to the 1981 census, the total population of Chotanagpur plateau is 17,601,969. It is unevenly distributed throughout the region ranging from 777.86 persons per sq km in Dhanbad Sadar subdivision to 100.54 persons per sq km in Latehar subdivision of Palamau district.

A cursory glance of the density map reveals that areas of comparatively higher density than the regions average (212 persons per sq km) are mostly confined within the river basins of Damodar including the Baraker, Subarnarekha and the South Koel.

It can be inferred that the degree of industrialisation and urbanisation and fertile levelled land are reflected in the high density of population.

Table 1
Population Density (1981)

Subdivision	*Density per square km*
1. Dumka	209.96
2. Jamtara	408.00
3. Deoghar	285.96
4. Godda	338.04
5. Rajmahal	384.71
6. Pakaur	257.07
7. Dhanbad	777.86
8. Baghmara	614.97
9. Giridih	237.47
10. Bermo	297.86
11. Hazaribagh	256.55
12. Chatra	124.83
13. Kodarma	202.06
14. Daltonganj	218.45
15. Latehar	100.54
16. Garhwa	150.03
17. Ranchi	385.50
18. Khunti	145.49
19. Simdega	107.52
20. Gumla	150.03
21. Lohardaga	115.26
22. Chaibasa	174.34
23. Seraikela	205.76
24. Dalbhum	390.27

The uneven distribution of population becomes even more pronounced when one goes below the regional level. The subdivisions recording very high density of population are Dhanbad (777.86), Baghmara (614.97), Jamtara (408), Dalbhum (390.27), Ranchi (385.50) and Rajmahal (384.71). The heavy concentration of population in these areas is partly due to development of mining and industrial centres and partly due to their levelled fertile agricultural land.

A high density of population is observed in Godda (338.04), Bermo (297.86), Deoghar (285.96), Pakaur (257.07), Hazaribagh (256.55) and Giridih (237.47). The location of mica mines and other services accounts for high density in Hazaribagh, Bermo, and Giridih Sadar subdivision while in Deoghar, Pakaurand Godda it is mainly due to suitable agricultural land.

Moderate density is found in Daltonganj (218.45), Dumka (209.96), Seraikela (205.76), Kodarma (202.06), Chaibasa (174.34) and Lohardaga (115.26).

The subdivisions recording low density of population are Garhwa (150.03), Khunti (145.49), Chatra (124.83), Gumla (150.03), Simdega (107.52) and Latehar (100.54). The reasons for low density in these areas are the infertile forested hilly tracts, eventually low supporting capacity of agriculture, poor communication facilities and other services.

Thus we can say that distribution of population in Chotanagpur is a reflection of the supporting capacity of the area. Hence, industrially and agriculturally developed areas have greater concentration of manpower, whereas hilly and forested infertile lands have relatively poor density.

GROWTH OF POPULATION

The Chotanagpur plateau has been recording continuous increase in its population except in the decade 1911-21, when the growth rate of its population remained stagnant. Over the span of 80, years the population of this region increased by 190 per cent which is slightly lower than the state average (194%). The growth has been very rapid during last the three decades with an increase of 19.68 per cent 22.58 per cent and 23.79 per cent in 1951-61, 1961-71 and 197.81 respectively. So far the highest growth rate was observed in the last decade. If we compare the average decennial growth rate of Chotanagpur plateau (24.06%) with different districts of this region, we find that districts recording higher growth rates than the state's average are Dhanbad (44.27%), Hazaribagh (36.36%), Giridih (25.98%) and Palamau (27..53%) while the remaining three districts, namely, Singhbhum (17.39%), Ranchi (17.58%) and Santhal Pargana (16.66%) have recorded lower growth rate. The main cause of higher growth rate in this region is large-scale immigration motivated by job opportunities in mining and industrial activities.

Before the planning period, the tribals of this region used to migrate to Assam and northern part of West Bengal where they easily got work in tea gardens. But after 1950-51, this trend of migration reversed. With the development of new industries and mines, not only was out-migration from this region stopped but also non-tribals from Bihar, and surrounding states and some districts of Bihar itself began to enter this region. The main source of their attraction has been economic opportunities found in this region.

When we take into account the dependency ratio[15] of Chotanagpur, it comes to 1.42 persons per worker. In other words we can say that 142 per cent of population of this region is dependent. The districts which record lower dependency ratio than the region's average (1.42%) are Singhbhum (1.26), Ranchi (1.24%) and Dhanbad (1.38%). These districts have lower dependency ratio because they are highly developed from the viewpoint of industries, transport, and other services. Other reasons for their low dependency ratio may be migration of workers especially male population from outside and secondly higher employment opportunities.

Table 2
Dependency Ratio, 1981

	Districts	*Workers* %	*Workforce* %	*Dependency ratio*
1.	Santhal Pargana	36.04	47.62	1.45
2.	Hazaribagh	33.98	45.82	1.59
3.	Giridih	34.04	46.63	1.56
4.	Dhanbad	30.01	54.04	1.38
5.	Ranchi	21.15	43.53	1.59
6.	Palamau	35.48	47.96	1.24
7.	Singhbhum	39.23	50.29	1.26
8.	Chotanagpur	36.34	48.15	1.42

The average working force of Chotanagpur plateau is 48.15 per cent. It means a little less than half of its total population is under working age group and unemployed. The districts having higher working force than the regions average are Singhbhum and Dhanbad. Though these districts have comparatively larger number of workers, yet there is high untapped workers owing to their high density of population.

FORESTRY

In spite of agriculture being the main source of livelihood of the people of Chotanagpur plateau, a large number of tribals of this region are engaged in forestry and its allied activities. It is commonly said that the culture of tribes originated and developed from hill and forest ecology. As forests are rapidly disappearing, the tribal economy based on forest also tends to decay. It is believed that when the region was completely wooded, there was naturally greater dependence on forest produce. Even nowadays the tribals such as the Hill Kharias, the Birhors and the Sauria Paharias who largely live in hilly and forested areas subsist on forest produce to a greater extent. Some of the tribal families fully earn their livelihood by selling firewood and other forest products in nearby towns.

It is important to note that tribals living in more remote and inaccessible areas have greater dependence on forestry and its allied activities. Though different types of forest acts have been imposed and preventive measures have been taken seriously, yet in practice it is impossible to restrict the tribals to enjoy the fruits of forest without changing their socio-cultural and economic life.

Among the districts of Chotanagpur plateau, the highest proportion of people engaged in forestry have been observed in Santhal Pargana (1.68%) closely followed by Giridih (1.59%), Palamau (1.50%), and Hazaribagh (1.44%). Ranchi district has witnessed the lowest proportion of only 0.50 per cent succeeded by Dhanbad (0.53%) and Singhbhum (1.0%).

MINING

The history of the modern economic development of Chotanagpur is the mainly history of the exploitation of its valuable mineral wealth. The plateau of Chotanagpur possessed numerous veins of minerals of various kinds which has been known to the local inhabitants for a long time. Iron-smelting tribes like Asur, Lohra, etc., were known as expert miners during the pre-industrial age. It was, however, during the beginning of this century that any systematic attempt was made to extract the minerals of this region. Today, Chotanagpur produces a major proportion of the total output of iron ore, manganese, coal, mica and several others minerals found in the country.

Mining and quarrying have taken place on a large scale in several areas and pockets, providing ample opportunities to registered employment under these activities. Moreover, the striking fact is that the aboriginals of the region (tribals) have not benefited much from these developments of modern specialised sector. In the matter of employment their claims have been skipped over. The data reveals that whereas 5.5 per cent of the total regional workforce was recorded in mining and quarrying activities, the corresponding figure for the tribal was as low as 1.66 per cent in 1971. As there is lack of training for the competent and skilled labourers, the local tribals could not claim much significant employment in this sector.

AGRICULTURE

In spite of large concentration of industries in Chotanagpur plateau, agriculture remains to be the mainstay of economy. According to the 1981 census, 68.86 per cent of the total workers are engaged in agriculture as against 79.06 per cent in Bihar. Nearly 29.56 per cent of the area was under cultivation in the year 1980-81 whereas cultivable land constitutes 57.89 per cent of the total area. Within the region there is significant variations in the area under cultivation. It is revealed in the table that only three districts, namely, Santhal Pargana (42.82) Ranchi (40.34%) and Singhbhum (30.14%) have higher percentage of net sown area than average for the Chotanagpur region. On the contrary, the percentage of net sown area is lower in the district of Palamau, Hazaribagh, Giridih and Dhanbad because their large part is either hilly and forested or under industrial and mining activities.

Table 3
Land Utilisation 1980-81

	Culturable Land %	*Net Sown Area %*	*Fallow Land %*	*Culturable Waste %*
Chotanagpur	57.8	29.569	21.95	4.32
Bihar	67.92	47.98	15.33	2.57

The proportion of fallow land in Chotanagpur is a little less than double of Bihar. A large area of culturable land is kept fallow every year owing to lack of moisture on uplands, inadequate water supply and poor soil.

Per capita cultivated land in Chotanagpur plateau is 0.13 hectare as against 0.11 hectare in Bihar. Due to low productivity of land, large areas have been brought under cultivation to cope with requirements. In the area of high density pressure on cultivated land is heavy. Added to it in industrial areas the percentage of cultivated land to the total area is quite low. Hence maximum pressure of population on cultivated land occurs in the areas comprising the subdivision of Dhanbad, Baghmara, Jamtara, Dalbhum, Ranchi and Rajmahal. In Palamau, Ranchi and Singhbhum districts due to low density of population and poor productivity the per capita cultivated land is higher than the region's average.

Table 4

Availability of Per Capita Cultivating Land

	Cultivated Land	*Persons*	*Per Capita Cultivated Land*
Santhal Pargana	693,000	3,717,528	0.01
Hazaribagh	229,000	2,198,310	0.08
Qiridih	174,000	1,731,462	0.08
Dhanbad	93,000	2,115,010	0.03
Ranchi	809,000	3,070,432	0.23
Palamau	218,000	1,917,528	0.10
Singhbhum	486,000	2,861,799	0.14
Chotanagpur	2,702,000	17,612,069	0.13
Bihar	5,404,000	69,914,734	01.11

Pressure on cultivated land can be released to some extent by utilising the culturable waste for agriculture. Culturable waste in Chotanagpur region accounts for only 8.40 per cent of the cultivable land as against 8.12 per cent in Bihar. With the inclusion of culturable waste, the pressure of population can be brought down to 4.28 persons per hectare from 7.47 person per hectare in the study area. Even then this land-man ratio will remain higher than the average in the north and eastern part of the region. The reason is that the area is very densely populated and any partial increase in the area under cultivation cannot decrease the pressure of population on land to any significant extent. The reverse is the case in Palamau. Hence the density of population is comparatively low and at the same time the percentage of culturable waste[16] to the cultivable land is also low. Hence the extension of cultivated land on the culturable land will lead to a remarkable decrease in the pressure of population with the provision of irrigation facilities, levelling and developing the culturable waste. Cultivated land can be raised to some extent thereby reducing the pressure of population on agricultural land to a limited extent.

Table 5

Percentage of Irrigated Land by Various Sources (1980-81)

Districts	*Canal*	*Tank*	*Well and Tubewell*	*Others*
1. Santhal Pargana	56.33	12.67	18.30	12.67
2. Hazaribagh	4.76	19.05	66.66	9.52
3. Giridih	7.14	7.14	71.43	14.28
4. Dhanbad	–	50.00	50.00	–
5. Ranchi	23.91	4.35	52.17	19.56
6. Palamau	13.11	8.20	27.87	50.82
7. Singhbhum	58.47	23.53	5.88	11.76
8. Chotanagpur	30.47	11.58	34.33	23.60

In the absence of perennial source of water almost all the irrigation facilities are seasonal. Important sources of irrigation in Chotanagpur are canals, tanks, wells, tubewells and other sources (Table-5). The sources of irrigation varies from region to region depending on topography, rainfall and geology. Canals are an important source of irrigation in river valleys like the lower Subarnarekha, the Damodar and Sankh basins. About 58.82 per cent of irrigated land gets water from canals in Singhbhum districts. Tanks are also important in the plain areas of Dhanbad and Singhbhum. In the hilly areas of Hazaribagh, Giridih and Ranchi wells and tubewells are the most important means of irrigation. Other sources of irrigation dominate in Palamau. The total irrigated area by different sources also varies at district level which may be seen in the Table 5. In the south and east part of Chotanagpur irrigation is least significant but towards the north-west it is well developed.

Table 6

Cropping Pattern 1980-81

Districts	*Rice*	*Wheat*	*Barley*	*Maize*	*Pulses*	*Others*
Santhal Pargana	78.52	4.54	0.78	0.09	3.44	3.73
Hazaribagh	69.91	4.25	1.59	12.76	1.06	10.33
Giridih	77.77	3.96	0.79	12.69	0.79	4.00
Dhanbad	68.18	1.13	1.13	6.81	13.66	9.09
Ranchi	89.73	2.43	0.17	2.72	3.29	1.38
Palamau	46.11	8.80	5.18	21.76	15.54	2.59
Singhbhum	94.97	2.56	2.38	00	00	00
Chotanagpur	81.17	3.51	0.87	7.72	4.30	2.40

The important crops grown in Chotanagpur are rice, wheat, maize, barley and pulses. It is revealed in Table 6 that rice is the predominant crop. It occupies the first position interms of area and production in almost all districts. Maize is the second ranking crop followed by pulses. The area under cultivation of rice is maximum in Singhbhum (94.97%), Ranchi (89.93%) and Santhal Pargana (78.52%). Maize occupies a relatively higher proportion of cultivated area of Palamau (21.76), Hazaribagh (12.76%) and Giridih (12.69%). The area under cultivation of barley is maximum in Palamau district. Agriculture of Chotanagpur plateau is extensive by nature, and thus, the production of foodgrains is not sufficient to meet the food requirement of the growing regional population. All the districts of the region are deficit in almost all foodgrains necessitating import. Generally, the import of foodgrains are made from immediate areas of south Bihar plain, where rice and other foodgrains are grown in surplus.

INDUSTRY

Chotanagpur is one of the most industrialised regions of India owing to abundance of forest and mineral raw materials, energy resources, dense network of transport and adequate labour force. On the basis of these facts it can be safely concluded that the development of this region very much depends on the progress of its industries although agriculture is the dominant economy of this region.

An appraisal of the spatial distribution of industries shows that the maximum agglomeration of industries both in number of units and employment is in the Subarnarekha and Damodar basins. North Koel basin has only a few industries. In the rest of the region industry is insignificant. Thus, industries are concentrated only at a few nodes. Location of industries has been guided by several factors. Metallic mineral-based and non-metallic mineral-based industries are confined to the Subarnarekha and Damodar basins respectively. Besides raw materials the industrial infrastructure is the most important pull factor in the location of industries. Metallic mineral and mineral-based industries have given preference to railways and even service industries have selected sites near roads. The eastern part of Chotanagpur has dense transportation network and is also connected with the territories outside the study area, and has the maximum industries. These river basins have also electric grid and coal reserves. Rivers supply water in plenty and also carry the affluent discharge of industries, thereby solving the problem of industrial waste disposal. Since these basins are well connected with Kolkata and Mumbai, they attracted enterpreneurs from outside. A maximum number of urban centres are also located in this area which also provide industries with infrastructure. These basins have also the advantage of a high density of population and therefore there is no dearth of manpower.

Within the industrial areas the distribution pattern of different types of industries varies. Some industries are localised, whereas others are less concentrated and well distributed.

Metallic mineral-based industries are concentrated in areas of extractive industries. This industry has clustered around selected nuclei in the Damodar and Subarnarekha basins. These clusters vary in their industry and character. Dhanbad and Sindri industrial cluster includes the nitrogen fertilizer factory of Sindri and the mining and machines building centres with specialisation in production of equipment for coal industry of Dhanbad. This area may extend up to the steel city of Bokaro in the near future.

The Jamshedpur industrial cluster comprises iron and steel plants and a number of related industries such as tin plate, electric cables and wires, locomotives, railway rolling stock, automobiles, paper machines, agricultural implements, earth moving machinery, heavy chemicals and refractories.

The Ranchi industrial cluster has Heavy Engineering Corporation, Ball Bearing Company, High Tension Insulator Factory, Heavy Machine Building Project, Foundry Forge Project, etc.

The fourth cluster is coming up in and around the Bokaro steel city. Industries of this area have come up taking advantage of railways.

Non-metallic mineral-based industries are also located near raw materials but are relatively scattered over the study area.

Mica manufacturing centres of Kodarma, Domchaneh and Tisri are in the mica belt. Giridih, an important industrial centre, lies outside the belt. Kodarma and Giridih are have railway lines.

The almunia manufacturing centre of Muri is located at a transportation node served by roads as well as by railways. It is also connected with the bauxite deposits of Lohardage through railways and roadways.

Copper deposits of economic size are found in Singhbhum. Ghatsila is the only manufacturer of refined copper ingots, copper sheets and brass sheets. It is located near the mining areas and is served by roads and railways.

Cement manufacturing centres are raw material-oriented. The cement plant of Jhinkpani, Japla and Khelari are dependent on limestone deposits of these districts. All these centres are near railway lines. The Sindri cement factory is based on the sludge waste of the fertiliser plant.

Agro-based industries are dispersed throughout Chotanagpur. Only in the Subrnarekha basin is there relatively large concentration of this type of industries due to higher agricultural productivity and good marketing facilities. In the North Koel and Damodar basins agro-based industries are relatively less developed. These are mostly small-scale industries.

Forest-based industries are distributed unevenly and are concentrated at a few favourable pockets in the Subarnarekha and North Koel basins.

The distribution pattern of different types of industries in relation to raw materials brings out the fact that along with agro-based and forest-based industries even the non-metallic mineral-based industries and to a limited extent the metallic-based industries can be located outside the emerging industrial areas. The first two types of industries can be well distributed in the western part of the region. In this way decentralised location of industries can be achieved, thus reducing spatial imbalance in industrial development.

TRANSPORT

The role of transport and communication in the socio-economic development of a region can hardly be overemphasised. Its chief function is to carry goods and people from one region to another. Indeed it is so important that it can truly be termed as the lifeline.

As regards, railway the study area is served by two zonal railways, i.e., the main lines of Eastern and South-eastern Railways.

i) The Grand Chord line of the Eastern Railway is a broad gauge double electrified line which runs from Howrah to Mughalsarai via Dhanbad and Gomoh.

ii) Barkakana loop broad gauge single line comes under South-eastern Railway. It joins the Grand Chord at Gomoh. The major coalfields of Raniganj, Katara and Giridih are interconnected by this line. The marshalling yard of Pathradih, Dhanbad and Patratu fall on this line.

iii) Ranchi district is served by the South-eastern Railway. The Muri-Ranchi-Hatia railway is broad gauge single line and Ranchi-Lohardaga route is narrow gauge. This route serves the bauxite deposits of Lohardaga, the industrial centres of Ranchi and connects it with the industrial centres of Damodar valley and Calcutta.

iv) In Singhghum district, the South-eastern Railway line bifurcates into several sections. From Muri to Chandil, there is a single broad guage line.

v) The line connecting Kolkata and Nagpur in Central Railway brings Tatanagar in contact with the steel plants of Rourkela and Bhilai. Its branch terminates at Gua. These are broad gauge double electrified lines.

vi) Tatanagar is again connected with Kharagpur industrial centres and the mining areas of Orissa.

The total length of railways in Chotanagpur comes to 1,351 km, i.e., for every 90 square kilometres there is an average of 1 km rail line. But railways are mostly confined to industrial areas. Dhanbad district is best served by railways in the region. Next comes Singhbbum district where towards the west, the length of railway per unit area decreases with undulating topography. Areas of high density obviously have longer route length, e.g., Dhanbad and Singhbhum are in better position than Palamau and Ranchi.

Next to railways, roads play a vital role as a means of transportation in the study area. Five per cent of the total area has roads complementary to railways. The Grand Trunk Road runs along the Grand Chord line. Similarly, the Ranchi-Latehar-Daltonganj road is parallel to the Barkakana loop. The Lohardaga-Muri Branch and all sections of the South-eastern Railway are complemented by roads. In Dhanbad also the railway lines have feeder roads. Out of the total available complementary roads, 49 per cent is in the Subarnarekha industrial area, 31 per cent in Damodar Basin and 20 per cent in the North Koel Basin.

The length of all motorable road per square km. of the area is 0.2 km. The industrial centres of Dhanbad, Hazaribagh and Palamau have greater lengths of road per unit area. But the road-man ratio is higher in the western part of the study area and in eastern Hazaribagh. This is due to the relatively low density of population.

Important industrial centres of Damodar valley and Subarnarekha basins are also served by the National Highway. NH-2 brings Dhanbad in contact with Burdwan, Asansol, Kolkata and Delhi. NH-32 originates at Gobindpur and goes to Jamshedpur via Purulia. NH-33 connects Hazaribagh, Ramgarh, Ranchi, Chaibasa and Jamshedpur with NH-2 and 6. Western Chotanagpur is not connected with the National Highway.

Road network is denser than that of railway. Hilly dissected topography accounts for it which stands in the way of construction of railways, but it is possible to construct roads as the permissible gradient is higher for the latter.

The quality of accessibility varies, 99 per cent of the study area is accessible. Among the industrial areas, Dhanbad district is the most accessible. The areas lying at a distance of more than 4 km from a road have not got proper accessibility and require attention. North-western Chotanagpur has maximum inaccessible areas as it has a highly dissected terrain with poor economy.

REFERENCES

1. Ahmad, E., *Bihar: A Physical, Economic and Regional Geography,* Ranchi University Ranchi, 1965, p. 24.
2. Prasad, A., "The Physical Landscope of Chotanagpur: A Study in Regional Geography", *Geographical Outlook*, p. 48.
3. Ibid., p. 46.
4. *District Gazetteers*, Santhal Parganas, Patna, 1938, p. 6.
5. Singly, R.L. (ed.) *India: A Regional Geography*, National Geographical Society of India, 1987, p. 672.
6. Dunn, J.A. and Dey, A.K., The Geology and Petrology of Singhbhum and surrounding areas, *Memories of Geological Survey of India,* vol. LXIX, Pt. 2, p. 328.
7. Singh, R.P., "Landscape of South-east Chotanagpur and Its Evolution", *The National Geographical Journal of India*, Vol. III, Pt. 3 & 4, 1957, p. 149.
8. A. Prasad, op.cit., p. 54.
9. Ram, L.N., "The Subarnarekha Basin in Bihar: A Study in Regional Geography", unpublished Ph.D. Thesis, Patna University, 1966, p. 54.
10. Cusec means cubic feet per second, i.e., the flow in one second is one cubic foot water.
11. Singh, R.L. op.cit., p. 654.
12. Dayal, P., *Bihar in Maps*, Patna, 1953, p. 16.
13. Ivern. F., *Chotanagpur Survey: a Study of Socio-Economic and Health Development,* New Delhi, 1959, p. 50.
14. Join Committee for Diagnostic Survey of Damodar Valley, *Synopsis of Interim Report*, Kharagpur, 1961.
15. Ratio between working and non-working population or number of dependent per worker.
16. Land suitable for agriculture but not under agriculture.

3

Identification of Indicators of Disparities

CONCEPTS OF INDICATORS

Though the term indicator has been often used in statistical literature, yet it has not been defined in a precise manner. Even standard dictionaries define it as something that indicates, shows or points out. The term has wider connotation than its literal meaning. "Indicators are not simply statistics and statistics are not 'ipso-facto' indicators unless some theory or assumption makes them so by relating the indicator variable as a phenomenon that it directly and fully measures."[1] Raymond A. Bauer, who was one of the main proponents of the social indicator movement, defines indicators as statistics, statistical series and other forms of evidences that enable us to assess where we stand and are going with respect to our values and goals, and to evaluate specific programmes and determine their impact.[2] Martin Kartzman views social indicator as a measurement of social phenomenon whose movement indicates whether a particular problem is getting better or worse relative to some goals.[3]

According to Doris Holleb social indicators are social measurements involving as assessment of social change in terms of explicit goals.[4]

Usually indicators are expressed in terms of ratios, proportions, averages, percentages, rates and other synthetic functions. The transformation of raw data into synthetic function is to eliminate the influence of population on any characteristics. It is therefore through an appropriate transformation of variables (which eliminates the effect on non-essential factors) within a theoretical format that an indicator can be formulated.

Indicator is considered synonymous with variable and index number but a careful observation may distinguish them. The term indicator has different connotations than variables. Jager supporting this view argues, "perhaps some variables should be treated as indicators while other should not, for if all variables were called indicators, there would have been no need of an additional term.[5]

Some of the distinctions between an indicator and a variable may be noted here. Indicators are generally expressed in terms of relative numbers while variables are in absolute numbers. Indicators make a general comment while variables make a specific comment. An indicator is a composite of at least two variables while a variable is a single entity.

An indicator, therefore can be defined as quantity which shows by its variations the changes over time or space of a magnitude which is not susceptible of direct observation in itself or direct observation in practice, while the index number generally conforms to a set form (or certain alternative forms). The indicator has apparently no such formulation, although it too often measures indirectly magnitudes which are not susceptible of direct measurement or observation and usually reflects more than what represents.[6]

A careful review of the above-mentioned definitions leads one to generic definition that social indicators are statistical measures which give information regarding social conditions and changes therein overtime for various segments of society. By social condition, we mean both external (social and physical) and the internal (subjective and perceptional) context of human existence. They are informational basis for decision makers, planners and researchers because most of the policies and programmes are formulated and implemented in the light of information gained from indicators. They help in achieving goals of planning. Some of these goals may be identification of backward regions and regional development and improvement of the standard of living.

Nowadays, a majority of developing nations give high priority to reducing social and economic inequalities and to suggest measure to improve the level of living of people below the poverty line in both forward and backward regions. The role of socio-economic indicators in the present context seems to be most crucial because they help in seeing two basic purposes : first, they assist in crystalising the goals of development planning in terms of specific objectives or targets, and second they help in measuring the progress made towards the goal in relation to the target fixed. Besides, they also serve a variety of other purposes like analysis of current situation of development, formulation of development policies, which can possibly be served by making use of these indicators, comprising analysis of main facets of well-being of the population, portrayal the state and trends in socio-economic conditions, which are likely to become the subject of public concern, crystallisation of the goals of development planning in terms of specific objectives, assessment of distribution of well-being and their role as critical variables in building development models. Thus one finds that socio-economic indicators can play a pivotal role in development planning in two ways. First, they can help in analysing the pre-plan socio-economic conditions and, secondly, they can assist in monitoring progress towards, development goals and providing information which facilitate formulations of policy and programmes and selection of priority areas. In this way they become an integral part of the planning process.

HISTORY OF THE EVOLUTION OF SOCIAL INDICATOR MOVEMENT

The movement to evolve social indicators on scientific lines has its origin back in 1929, when a group of social scientists were invited by Herbert Hoover, the then President of United States, to discuss the proposal of a national survey for analysing social trends.[7] However, the actual work was initiated in 1962 when the Academy of Arts and Sciences undertook a project for National Aeronatics and Space Administration. The main objective of this project was to assess the impact of space programmes on American society. The findings of the project were published in a book entitled *Social Indicators* edited by Raymond A. Bauer who was one of the main exponents of the indicator movement in its early stage of development.[8] The government of the United States strengthened the movement by official declaration to establish a system of social accounts, which deals with cost benefit analysis of some more areas than what were already covered by the National Income Accounts.

The next development which occurred in the indicator movement was Ogburn tradition of measuring social trends. It was started in 1966 by Wilburt E. and Elenor Berner Sheldon. They contributed a paper entitled of *Monitoring Social Change: A Conceptual and Pragmatic Statement*. In this paper they attempted to define the concept of social change as structural transformation. They also pointed out certain areas to examine social change. On the basis of the framework proposed by them a book was edited by Sheldon and Moore in 1968. The title of the book was *Indicators of Social Change*. It was considered to be the most comprehensive work on social indicators of recent social trends in the major dimensions of American society.[9]

The United States Department of Health, Education and Welfare released a seminal document entitled 'Toward A Social Report' which is considered as the most important event in the history of social indicator movement. It developed interest among professionals as well as ordinary people toward the indicator movement. The document explores a variety of measures that can help to monitor the changing social conditions in several areas (health and illness, social mobility, physical environment, income and property, public order and safety, learning science and arts and participation and alienation). It also discusses the availability and utility of indicators, sets out criteria for the choice of indicators and argues that these are necessary requisites for the development of a comprehensive social report that would give a detailed image of social life.[10]

Publication of *Toward A Social Report* was stopped after a few years. However work on social indicators continued at the federal government level. A major achievement of the federal government in this direction is the publication of social indicators in 1974. It contains statistics reflecting social conditions and trends in United States. It focuses attention on eight major social aspects such as health, public safety, housing, education, employment, income, leisure, recreation and population.

Pioneering work on social indicators in France is credited to Jaques Delores. His work entitled *Les Indicateurs Sociaux* was published in 1968.[11] It gives information on various aspects of French society and stimulates researchers and government agencies to construct social indicators. Similarly, in Germany, Norway, Sweden and Canada a number of statistical volumes have been produced. Thus the 'Social indicator' movement which began in the United States in the mid-1960's has since spread across both Atlantic and Pacific.[12]

There is now a strong interest in developing social indicators at the national level in many other countries. It was United Kingdom which began work on indicators after USA. The pioneering work on social indicators is *Great Britain is Social Trend* whose first volume was published in 1970.

In Japan the Sanwa Bank has attempted to compare national well-being with that of other advanced industrial nations by means of a "happiness index".

POSITION OF INDICATORS IN INDIA

Major sources of information on various socio-economic aspects of society in India are the Census Organisation, the Central

Statistical Organisation, the National Sample Survey, the Planning Commission and the Indian Council of Social Science Research. Besides these, departments and ministries like Health, Education, Rural Development, Agriculture and Industry compile data in their related field.

The Census Organisation of India is the most important government agency which produces data covering a wide range of socio-economic conditions. The census operation in India is undertaken once in 10 years. The data available from census includes demographic attributes such as population distribution, growth, density, age and sex composition and migration. It also provides data on literacy, educational attainment, workers in different activities and houseless population. Apart from decennial census, some specific studies are also conducted to compile information on infant mortality ratio, birthrate, deathrate, and fertility by sample registration survey.

Initially the National Sample Survey was constituted for collecting information on national income estimates but now it has diversified its activities. It is actively engaged in compilation of data related to health, housing, education, employment, and unemployment, land-holding, etc.

The data collected by this organisation on population characteristic are in the cycle of 10 years whereas that of employment and unemployment have a gap of five years.

The Central Statistical Organisation which forms an integral part of the Ministry of Planning and is closely associated with the activities of Planning Commission. It is responsible for coordination of statistical activities in the country, maintenance of statistical standard, conducting economic surveys, plan works related to development of statistics and dissemination of plan work.

The Planning Commission is a supra-level agency responsible for formulation of policies and plants at the national level. It develops indicators for pre-plan analysis of situation and its post-plan assessment.

The Indian Council of Social Science Research is also one of the main research institutes in the country which plays a vital role in the development of socio-economic indicators.

CHARACTERISTICS OF INDICATORS

A good indicator should have the following characteristics:

1. It should be closely related to the situation and always be objective-oriented.
2. It should be brief and serve as key indicator.
3. It should be unique and clearly understandable.
4. It should be designed to measure the effects of policies, plans, programmes and major goals of economic and social development.
5. It should be indicative of current trends and be useable for current analysis.
6. It should be sensitive so that small changes in areal unit could be reflected in the value of the indicator.
7. It should be available as a time series.
8. It should be easily disaggregated by geographical areas.
9. As to feasibility, the value of the indicator should easily be workable and information should not pose any problem.
10. It should be relatable to public policy and goals, such as equal opportunity, public order and safety.
11. It should be stable so that comparable value can be obtained over-time and space. In other words, the data element used in its definition should not change their meaning over time, space and agency.

SELECTION OF INDICATORS

Selection of indicators constitutes the crux of methodology because with the help of it pertinent questions are asked.

However, their selection is a very complex task which requires a lot of cares.

The first and foremost consideration regarding selection of indicators is that only those indicators should be chosen which are relevant to the nature of problem and are easily available at different points of time. The use of irrelevant indicators fails to project a real image of the situation. For example, if one intends to measure levels of disparities and make use of indicators of diversity, his research findings will reflect the level of diversity rather than disparity. The selection of indicators without taking care of their appropriateness, availability and frequency generally creates a lot of problems.

There is no rigid rule as regards the number of indicators used. However, social scientists and planners prefer a short list of indicators which may present a summary view of the socio-economic situation. Selection of too many indicators without combining them in groups or in aggregate cannot reveal the actual socio-economic conditions. On the other hand, the use of few indicators gloss over the important trends which are to be noted. Therefore, as a compromise, there should be a key indicator from each sector reflecting the progress towards major goals and one or two more supplementary indicators to show the trends.[13]

An integrated system of indicators should include all types of socio-economic indicators pertaining to different sector of economy. However, in case, the choice is of the phenomenon measured to the setting or background in which it takes place. The limitation of basic measures is that it cannot indicate anything more than absolute number unless related with the area and population. Its use may be meaningfully taken as time series or series of comparable or related figures and relationship to be derived by readers.[14]

Social indicators have been grouped under the following heads:

1. Health
2. Housing and environment

3. Education
4. Security
5. Level of urbanisation

Similarly, economic indicators have been categorised as under:

1. Size of land holding
2. Occupational status
3. Level of agricultural development
4. Level of industrial development

HEALTH

Health and nutrition are essential aspects of the level of living, and their significance as an indicator of social and economic inequality hardly needs any elaboration. Health is fundamental to personal happiness and the ability to enjoy and appreciate all other aspects of life, and has a strong influence on productivity and earning capacity. A healthy person is not only happy but also enjoys life more.

The term health has been defined in different ways by various scholars and organisations. According to the World Health Organisation (WHO) health is a state of complete physical, mental and social well-being and not merely the absence of disease and infirmity.[15] Taleoft Parensons emphasised that, the indicator should be development oriented and directly concerned with major goals of socio-economic development. Sometimes such goals might involved structural changes, in such circumstances, the indicators reflecting structural changes should be preferred. In case, goals involve changes in certain flows, flow indicators should be used. The progress made in social services should be measured in terms of benefits derived by the population. However, in the absence of the data of benefits derived, the progress might be measured in terms of output indicators. Even if the data of output indicators are not available, input indicators would be better alternatives.[16]

The choice of indicator must be in a defined analytical framework. It can be done by personal judgement but it may be arbitrary and biased. Therefore, statistical techniques like factor analysis should be preferred to determine weights of selected indicators and identify basic factors which are crucial for the development of the key sector of economy.[17]

Indicators may be used both in terms of basic measures and derived figures. The use of derived figures such as percentages ratios, proportions, etc., reflects relationships defines' health as is optimum capacity of an individual for effective performance of the role and task for which he has been socialised. Thus, health is a state of soundness of mind and body of an individual in which he is free from any sort of disorder, pain or sickness, and all organs of body function well and are conducive to an efficient and prolonged life.

Health is influenced by a number of factors such as nutrition, health care facilities, sanitation, drinking water, housing and environment. However, only nutrition and health care facilities have been taken into consideration here, other factors have been considered separately. The selected indicator of health care includes hospitals and dispensaries, hospital beds, and doctors per million of population. The high value of these indicators are a sign of good health and vice versa. The rational for selecting hospitals and dispensaries per million of population is that there is a provision of free medical care and their availability is most essential in the study area, where the majority of population is poverty-striken and cannot bear the expenses of treatment. Availability of hospitals does not mean that they have adequate number of doctors and beds serving the need of population. Doctors and beds per million of population have been taken as separate indicators. The proportion of doctors in relation to population is an indication of how population is served by doctors, whereas the number of beds per million of population reflects facilities available for the treatment of patients who need special care in hospitals.

HOUSING AND ENVIRONMENT

The study of social and economic inequalities seems to be incomplete without considering housing and environment, because it is a basic human need after food and clothes. It has a greater bearing on health, productivity and income of an individual. Burns[18] advocates indirect benefits of good housing as : (1) increased work productivity, (2) improved health, (3) increased effectiveness of educational efforts, and (4) reduction in crime, juvenile deliquency and other forms of social deviance. While direct benefit of housing is that it provides shelter and protection from constraint of weather, it would be worthwhile to clear the concept of housing before discussing its various aspects. Based on common characteristics, housing may be defined as a physical structure which provides shelter and a package of services to its occupants. It is also an economic good, a capital stock, a status symbol and a political hot potato.

According to the 1981 Census, a house is a building having a separate main entrance from the road or common courtyard or staircase, etc., used or recognised as a separate unit. Though housing is one of the basic human needs, millions of people, specially in the third world, are living under highly inhuman conditions of deprivation. Overcrowding, lack of privacy, total absence or inadequacy of basic amenities and use of substandard building materials dominate the housing scene. The problem of housing exists both in rural and urban areas but it is more acute in the latter which may be attributed to the fast growth of urbanisation. The rate at which houses are built, lags far behind the rate at which urban population is increasing due to lack of land and high cost of building materials. The indicator of percentage of houses to the total population has been selected to show conditions of prevailing poverty and inequality in terms of housing. Generally it has been observed that people living in abject poverty do not have their own house to live in. They spend their life either in an open environment or in slums or squatters settlement. On the other hand, rich and affluent people have decent houses with access to all types of luxuries and comforts.

Housing congestion is also a manifestation of poverty. People with low income have to accommodate themselves in houses which are not adequate for them. Excessive crowding has been found to have a deteriora impact not only on the condition of health but to a larger extent also on distortion of social and physiological values, specially of children. It not only makes children devoid of the sense of individuality and self-sufficiency, but even among adults, it often causes irritability and flashes of violence. Housing congestion leads people to move out to streets, thus breaking up fragile family ties.

The percentage of pucca houses to the total houses has been taken into consideration in order to show the physical quality of houses which reflects the socio-economic status of their occupants. It is generally observed that the will-to-do persons live in decent houses in posh localities whereas poor person are either houseless or live in dilapidated shocks, slums and squatter settlement or on roadsides.

The physical quality of houses has been categorised on the basis of materials used in the construction of roofs and walls. Based on the types of building material used, two types of houses—'*kuccha*' and '*Pucca*'—can be identified. The former has walls made of grass, leaves, reeds or bamboos, etc., while the latter type is one which has walls made mainly of burnt bricks, G.I. sheets or other metal sheets, stones, cement, concrete, etc., while roof materials include brick and lime, stone, concrete, RBC and RRC, etc.

Thus in terms of building material used in the two categories of houses, no ambiguity as to the cost and quality of construction of house is left. Pucca houses, being an indication of the high standard of living, their spatial dimensions displays the disparity in the level of housing conditions. Although, house types based on materials used is largely a function of the availability of materials and nature of the physical environment, yet with rapid rate of communication development and invention of scientific gadgets to overcome extremes of climatic hazards, the excuse of poor housing due to non-availability of raw materials is unjustified. However, it is an established fact that house type is a function of economic status, which to a larger extent also corresponds to its social status.

EDUCATION

Education is a crucial factor of economic, social, and cultural development. It provides economic opportunities and helps to overcome social barriers. It also enhances earning potential and productivity of people through acquisition of skills and information for various opportunities and jobs. Thus education determines the quality of people and the development of a region.

The significance of education in the present study is utmost because it acts as a leveller of social and economic inequalities. It is education that contribute significantly in improving the condition of people from a state of deprivation to prosperity. "Education not only yields a huge set of benefits to individual concerned as well as to the society in the form of a larger set of externalities but it also regarded as a great equaliser in improving income distribution and reducing poverty and inequalities."[19]

Studies made by Tilak[20] have proved that there is positive relationship between education and earning both at the macro and the micro level. The study reveals that education alone explains more than 30 per cent and education together with experience about 50 per cent of the variances of the individual earnings in South Indian district.

Oberai and Singh[21] observed that the earning of an individual varies with the level of his educational attainment. They concluded in their study that in the Punjab plain the earnings of graduates and above exceeds those with no formal education or those who are illiterate by 40 per cent.

Besides improving the economic condition of people, education also determines their social status. Usually highly educated people are placed at the higher ladder of social hierarchy and vice versa. Socio-economic survey on caste/communities undertaken by the Kerala Bureau of Economics and Statistics suggests that there is also a close link between relative position in social hierarchy and educational level attained by people.[22]

Levels of educational development can be assessed both with the help of flow indicators and stacks indicators. In the present study levels of educational development have been measured using stock indicators such as percentage of literates to the total population at Primary schools, Middle schools and High schools level. Inclusion of these indicators are based on availability of data. The study area, Chotanagpur, is one of the backward regions of India where illiteracy and ignorance is widely spread. In such a state removal of mass illiteracy will be a panacea for overall development of the people. The significance of literacy lies in the fact that it forms the basis of multi-level educational pyramid. Literacy opens the door of various opportunities and enables people to avail them. A literate person can distinguish between right and wrong and take the right decision, owing to the vital role which literacy plays in the socio-economic upliftment of people. The founding fathers of Indian Constitution recommended that it be made free and compulsory. The universalisation of literacy and primary education has been recognised as one of the major goals of planning.

Hence the percentage of literates to the total population has been selected as an important indicator.

SECURITY

Crime is a social evil on account of which life and property of people are at risk. In a region of high incidence of crime, there is a feeling of fear and insecurity among individuals, which adversely affects their quality of life. Crime and social security has been incorporated in this study because they have a direct bearing on a happy and peaceful life.

The causes of crime may be environmental, social and psychological but the most important cause is economic. Most of the crimes, directly or indirectly, are committed for economic gain. The inequalities between haves and have nots stimulate the poor to commit crime for meeting their necessities, while the love of riches give birth to many other crimes. Thus most of the crimes are economically motivated, and poverty and inequalities are highly conducive to it.

The domain of crime and social security is very wide, however, only one aspect of social security, e.g. police per million of population has been considered.

This indicator has been chosen for showing spatial variations of security facilities in this context of the prevailing crime situation.

Though data pertaining to the number of police stations in each district are available, mere presence of police stations does not necessarily imply in the Indian context, the availability of adequate security. It is a well-known fact that many police stations especially in rural areas, are not only woefully understaffed but lack even elementary facilities for crime detection and enforcement of law and order.

LEVEL OF URBANISATION

The level of urbanisation is considered to be an indicator of industrialisation, modernisation and economic development. It not only improves the economic condition of people but also changes their lifestyle. In India the old tradition of caste and joint family systems have been weathering away as a consequence of urbanisation. Sharma[23] established the relationship between degree of urbanisation and the level of economic development in Chotanagpur plateau by telescoping the effect of urbanisation in the perspective of industrial development, creation of sectoral employment and generation of sectoral per capita income. He finds urbanisation and per capita income to be positively correlated.

Geographers define urbanisation in relation to distribution of urban spaces and the proportion of urban population to the total population. It implies that an increase in both the above attributes at a given time is an indication of the growth of urbanisation and vice versa. According to the Census of India, a place must fulfil the following criteria to be considered as an urban centre : (1) It must have a density of population not less than 1,000 person per square mile. (2) It must have at least a total population of 5,000 persons. (3) Three-fourths of the population must be engaged in non-agricultural activities.

In an underdeveloped country with traditional social structure which is going through a process of socio-economic change under conditions of political democracy, free migration of population has wider economic, political and cultural dimensions. Internal migration, induced by small, isolated pockets of prosperity in a country in which basic development is extremely uneven in spatial terms, has perverse effect of accentuating regional inequality. There is overwhelming evidences that the countryside expels not necessarily the most efficient and enterprising workers but vast masses of landless peasants and marginal farmers who are unable or unwilling to carry on as floating labourers in rural areas. When they flock to cities they create a spurious type of urbanisation which has a danger potent for economic, social and political instability. The emergence of such cities, towns and growth centres therefore, has to own socio-economic implications. No doubt urbanisation brings change in development processes but at the same time also creates regional instability.

Urbanisation represents a revolutionary change in the whole pattern of social life. Itself a product of basic economy and technological developments, it tends, in turn, once it comes into being, to affect every aspect of existence. The traditional concepts, values and functions become very weak under the influence of urbanisation. Thus urbanisation may be regarded as one of the agents of social change. As observed by Sjoberg[24] "the relationship between urbanisation and social change is too complex, involves and ramified to be accounted for interm of simple one-sided causal nexus."

In the present study the proportion of urban population of the total population has been taken as an indicator of urbanisation. The significance of urbanisation is that it involves the movement of people out of agricultural activities into other non-agricultural, industrial and service sectors. The social significance of urbanisation is also portrayed by better facilities provided in the form of educational and medical institutions, and banking facilities which result in the wide disparities in patterns of rural urban living.

SIZE OF LAND HOLDING

The size of a land holding is one of the important factors influencing agricultural development and thus determining the socio-economic status of the people of any region. It is more so in an essentially agricultural country like India, where land being scarce, is much valued by people. There are two contradictory views regarding the size of holding and agricultural development which is, in fact, a result of adoption of agricultural innovations. According to one group of scholars there is a positive and high correlation between the extent of land ownership and adoption of agricultural innovation by farmers due to many reasons. Firstly, many innovations such as new agricultural implements, tractor, pumping set, thresher, etc., require substantial capital which is beyond the capital resource of smaller cultivators. Secondly, the adoption of innovation is a matter of risk. Thirdly, many innovations such as tractors, power sprayer, power duster and harvestor can be used economically in contiguous and large strip of fields. On the other hand, there are others who believe that smaller farmers adopt improved agricultural practices much earlier than bigger ones because small farmers due to low income and yield are highly motivated to increase the level of living by adopting new methods of cultivation as compared to the large size farmer who generally does not feel the necessity so intensively to raise his overall agricultural output.

OCCUPATIONAL STATUS

The occupational structure of a society is one of the good indicators of social and economic inequality because to a large extent, it determines the level of living standard. The study intended to understand the pattern of inequality should, therefore, gives due attention to this feature. In addition to providing an insight into the nature of economy it also throws light on the socio-economic, cultural and political condition of society.

For instance, the proportion of workers engaged in secondary and tertiary sectors is an indicator of development, whereas that in the agricultural sector is indicative of comparative underdevelopment. This is due to the fact that value added by manufacturing and services sectors are higher than that in the agricultural sector. That is why the percentage of workers depending on manufacturing and tertiary sectors is very high in developed countries but it is very low in developing countries. Clark observes that a rise in per capita income is accomplished by a decline in the proportion of workers in agriculture and an increase in manufacturing and service activities. Thus changes in the composition of workforce reflects change in the economy of a region. For instance, a movement of workers from the agricultural sector to secondary and tertiary sectors implies greater economic development and a higher level of well being. Despite its limitation in comprehending all forces determining the comparative contribution of economic activities to the regional development, workforce provides the only uniform basis for measuring and comparing the distribution, volume and types of economic activities which are indicators of economic development. In this way workforce is a better measure of the relative levels of development than income per capita, value added or value of products. Comparison overtime based on these indicators would be distorted if changes in price level took place.

In the present study percentages of agricultural and non-agricultural works in the total workforce have been selected as indicators to show the nature of economy and the level of living in different parts of the state.

LEVEL OF AGRICULTURAL DEVELOPMENT

Agriculture plays an important role in the overall development as it provides food surplus to the growing population, raw material to agro-based industries, employment to rural population and improves their standard of living. According to Organisation for Ecoinomic Co-operation and Development (OECD) group of experts,[25] agriculture can contribute to growth by increasing the efficiency of production and releasing resources to other sectors by adjusting the composition and of agricultural production in proportion with the growth in internal and external demands,

1. By the transfer of resources, labour and capital from agriculture to other sectors of the economy, thus contributing to overall growth if the productivity of factors transfer is higher outside the agricultural sector than within it.
2. By contributing to the supply of foreign exchange and the balance of payments, to the extent that the export of scale of output to demand continuing and substantial adjustments in agricultural technology, in the structure of the industry and in the composition and cost of farm output are in the long run the basis for agriculture's

contribution to the well balanced and rapid growth in the economy. Furthermore, agriculture can contribute to overall development in many ways.

3. By increasing the volume of agricultural products exceeding imports. The foreign currency obtained from net export can be used to import of the capital goods needed to modernise the economy.
4. By contributing to the process of industrialisation either through the supplying raw materials for the agriculture industries or through purchasing industrial goods, thus stimulating the process of industrialisation and overall growth.[26]

   Rising agricultural productivity supports and sustains industrial development in several important ways, firstly to permit agriculture to release part of its labour force for industrial employment while meeting the increasing food needs of the non-agricultural sectors. Secondly it raises agricultural incomes, thereby creating the rural purchasing power needed to buy the new industrial goods and rural savings, which may then be mobilised by direct or indirect means to finance industrial development. Finally it enables agriculture to supply the major wage goods (food) of industrial workers at prices favourable to the profitability of new industry.
5. Agricultural development also brings social and cultural developments, as increased per capita income in rural areas invariably results in increased literacy and level of education which are conducive to social transformations.

It is clear that under all circumstances agricultural productivity makes important contribution to regional development and that within considerable limit at least it is one of the preconditions which must be established before a take-off into self-sustained economic growth becomes possible. It is equally clear that social and cultural change necessary to assimilate new industrial and technological development is possible through increased agricultural production.[27]

Agricultural development can be measured both in terms of input such as seeds, fertilisers, irrigation, mechanisation, etc., as well as output like productivity.

In the present study agricultural productivity has been taken as a measure of agricultural development because it is the outcome of a number of inputs. If both input and output are taken into account, it will be duplication of information.

LEVEL OF INDUSTRIAL DEVELOPMENT

The role of industries in the economic development of any region is undeniable. Industrialisation is a key force of rapid development of any economy. Most of the economists have accepted industrialisation as the most dominant component of their development strategies. Industrial units of organising sectors generally provide life blood to the economic system by their leading role in transmitting growth impulses to the surrounding areas through their backward and forward linkages. Most of the infrastructure, such as means of transportation, power and banking expands along with industrial development while their availability in the area causes concentration of industries. Industrialisation not only provides employment opportunities and reduces the dependence of workforce on agriculture but also acts as an agent of socio-cultural transformation by bringing about urbanisation and modernisation.

There is a great degree of association between industrialisation and urbanisation and both of them move side by side in the same direction. If one tries to explain, the genesis of urbanisation finds that as soon as a new manufacturing plant is located in a rural area it gives rise to trade, commerce and transport activities. It also further attracts many more allied industries in that area due to certain locational advantages.

Hence people in large proportion get jobs in these non-agricultural activities, the economy of the area is transformed and thus urbanisation starts from industrial development.

Kuznets[28] observed positive and marked association of urbanisation, industrialisation and per capita income at the international level. He found that in almost all advanced countries which are highly industrialised there is a high degree of urbanisation and high per capita income and vice-versa. A balance explanation of the connection of industrialisation and per capita income is that industrially developed countries are able to exploit their economic potentials by higher technology in almost all sectors which produce high return.

It is a serious misnomer that industrial development is paramount and the only means of economic upliftment. No doubt, the most advanced countries are the ones which are the best developed industrially, but the basis of industrial development lies in agriculture and a balance between the two is essential for the achievement of economic progress and to avoid structural disequilibrium which may be a source of hardship. Besides, agricultural output it also provides the "basic working capital for industrialisation."[29]

LIST OF INDICATORS

1. Hospitals/10,000 of population
2. Public health centres/100,000 of population
3. Beds/100,000 of population
4. Doctors/100,000 of population
5. Percentage of pucca houses/total houses
6. Percentage of houseless/total population
7. Drinking water
8. Percentage of electrified villages/total villages
9. Percentage of literates/total population

10. Primary schools/100,000 of population
11: Middle schools/100,000 of population
12. Secondary schools/100,000 of population
13. Percentage of urban population/total population
14. Police/100,000 of population
15. Percentage of main workers/total population
16. Percentage of non-agricultural workers/total workers
17. Percentage of small and marginal land holding/total holding
18. Percentage of net sown area/total area
19. Agricultural productivity per hectare (in Rs.)
20. Factories/10,000 of population.

REFERENCES

1. Rao, M.V.S., "Socio-economic indicators for Development" in *National Seminar on Social Statistics*, C.S.O, vol.I, Applied Publication, New Delhi, 1977, p. 169.
2. Bauer, R.A., *Social Indicator*, MIT Press Cambridge,1966.
3. Quoted by Rao, M.V.S. *Indicators of Human and Social Development*, HSDPD-8/UNUP-10, p. 78.
4. Ibid., p. 78.
5. Quoted in the *International Encyclopedia of Education*, volume 5, Pergamon Press, 1985, p. 2433.
6. Rao, M.V.S., Socio-economic indicators for development planning, in *The Use of Socio-economic Indicators in Development Planning*, UNESCO, 1979, pp. 90-91.
7. Kundu, A., *Measurement of Urban Processes: A Study in Regionalisation*, Bombay, 1980, p. 29.
8. Land Kenneth, C., "Theories, models and indicators of Social Change", *International Social Science Journal*, vol. XXVII, No.l, 1975, p. 9.
9. Land, Kenneth, C., op.cit., p. 10.
10. Knox, P.L., *Social Well-Being : A Spatial Perspective Theory and Practice in Geography*, Oxford University Press, 1975, pp. 8-9.

11. Land, Kenneth, C., op.cit., p. 11.
12. Knox, P., L., op.cit., pp. 88-.89.
13. Rao, M.V.S., op.cit., p. 101.
14. Rao, M.V.S., op.cit., p. 101.
15. Friedlander, W.A. and Apte, R. Z. *Introduction to Social Welfare*, New Jersey: Prentice Hall Pub., 1980, p. 364.
16. Rao, M.V.S., op.cit., p. 93.
17. Tewari, R.T., *Changing Pattern of development in India*, Ashish Publishing House, New Delhi, 1984, p. 34.
18. Bourne, L.S., *The Geography of Housing*, Edward Arnold, 1984, pp. 13-14.
19. Nair, K.R.G. (ed.), *Regional Disparities in India*, Agricole Publishing Academy, New Delhi, 1981, p. 34.
20. Tilak, J.B.G., (ed.), *Education and Regional Development*, Yatna Publications, New Delhi, 1986, p. 134.
21. Ibid., p. 134.
22. Oberai, A.S. and Singh, H.K.M., *Causes and Consequences of Internal Migration*, Oxford University Press, 1983, p. 287.
23. Sharma, N., "Degree of Urbanisation and Level of Economic Development in Chotanagpur : A Study in Nature of Relationship", *Indian Journal of Regional Science*, vol. IV, No. 2, 1972, pp. 143-154.
24. Sjoberg, G., "The Pre-Industrial city" in Halt, P.K. and Reiss, A.J. (eds.), *Cities and Society*, New York Press, pp. 13, 331-42.
25. *Agriculture and Economic Growth—A Report by a Group of Experts Organisation for Economic Co-operation and Development*, Paris, 1985, p. 23.
26. Lewis, W.A., *Theory of Economic Growth*, London, 1955, p. 334.
27. Malassis, L. *Education and Rural Development*, 3, UNESCO, Paris, 1975, pp. 20 and 41.
28. Kuznets, S. Consumption industrialisation and urbanisation, in Horelitz, H.F, and Moore, W.E. (Ed.) *Industrialisation and Society*, UNESCO, Mouton, 1970, p.102.
29. Rostow, W.W., The noted American economist and author of The Stages of Economic Growth, in his lecture on "Nationalism and Take off", delivered at the Institute of Economic Growth, New Delhi, April 1963.

4

Patterns of Social and Economic Disparities

The present chapter is an attempt to measure spatial patterns of social and economic disparities in Chotanagpur plateau. An analysis of regional disparities provides a base for a regional planning. Such type of studies help researchers, administrators, policy makers and planners in identifying regions at different levels of development, both in sectoral and aggregate terms and to suggest suitable strategies for their development. Thus measurement of disparities in terms of the regional dimension is one of the essential prerequisites for balanced development because it provides guidelines at the time of formulating plans for backward area development.

This chapter intends to test the hypothesis that marked regional disparities occurs in the study area. The main objective of such an endeavour is to suggest strategies for minimising disparities if they exist.

Socio-economic disparities have been measured by using the statistical technique of Standard Score Additive Model. Data have been processed in the computer. The Z-score is a linear transformation of the original data in such a way that its mean becomes '0' and its standard deviation becomes unity. For observation 'i' on any variable, the standard score (Z_i) is given by:

$$Z_i = \frac{X_1 - \bar{X}}{S}$$

where

X_1 is the original value for observation

$\bar{X}$ is the mean for variable and

S is the standard deviation.

The Standard Scores Additive Model has been used to develop a composite social and economic indicator for each of the nine major groups of indicators shown above and the overall socio-economic conditions including all sets of variables. The nine sets of indicators require the addition of the Z-score for the individual variables taken to measure them. The model is thus:

$$I_J = \sum_{i=1}^{K} Z_i J$$

I_J is the magnitude of the indicator for the sub-division 'J'. Z^iJ is the standard score on variable (i) in the subdivision 'J'. 'K' is the number of variables measuring the criterion in question being a subset of the total 'm' variables.

The overall general indicator of social and economic disparity (SED) for any subdivision will be

$$SED = \sum_{i=1}^{m} ZiJ$$

or in this case

$$SED = \sum_{i=1}^{20} ZiJ$$

The standardised scores have been divided into five grades (class intervals) of very high, high, medium, low and very low. The high scores are more than +1.5 standard deviation from the mean (O). The category of high scores range is from +1.5 to +.5 standard deviation. The medium grade of Z-scores ranges from +.5 to -5 standard deviation. The Z-scores ranging from -.5 to -1.5 standard deviation are categorised in low grade. The subdivisions having the scores less than -1.5 are categorised as very low grade.

Table 7 shows spatial patterns of disparity in terms of a set of indicators pertaining to health facilities. It is clear from the table that health facilities are very high (2.55) in only one subdivision, namely, Latehar. The subdivisions recording high health facilities are Chatra (1.10), Baghmara (1.00), Lohardaga (1.10) and Gumla (0.71). All these subdivisions do not form a compact region except Lohardaga and Gumla.

Four regions of medium health facilities may be observed which are scattered in the east, west, south and central part of the study area. The eastern region of medium health facilities comprises Godda (-0.16), Pakaur (0.14) and Dumka (0.00) while the western region consists of Garhwa (-0.04) and Daltonganj (-0.07). The central region of medium health facilities includes Kodarma (0.28), Giridih (-0.15), Dhanbad (-0.26), Hazaribagh (0.44) and Ranchi (0.12), while the southern region comprises Simdega (0.38), Chaibasa (0.39), Seraikela (-0.06) and Dalbhum (-0.09).

Only three subdivisions come under the grade of low health facilities. These are Barmo (-1.40), Rajmahal (-1.25) and Khunti (-0.62). There is a very small region of very low health facilities comprising Deoghar (-1.54) and Jamtara (-2.55) which is located in the east.

Regional pattern of disparity as regards a group of indicators of housing and environment at a glance gives an impression that three subdivisions, namely, Baghmara (1.66), Daltonganj (1.93) and Dalbhum (2.09) record very high scores of housing and environment. The scores of housing and environment are high in Chatra (0.62), Hazaribagh (0.83), Ranchi (0.93) and Chaibasa (0.60). These together make a large compact region but Dhanbad and Chaibasa lie further apart.

Two distinct regions of medium level of development of housing and environment have been observed. One is located in the western part consisting of Kodarma (0.17), Latehar (2.55), and Lohardaga (0.48). The other region lies in central part and consists of Kodarma (0.29), Giridih (-0.17), and Bermo (0.03).

Similarly, there are also two regions of low level of development of housing and environment which are located in the southern and extreme eastern part of the study area. They include Gumla (-1.20), Simdega (-1.06), Khunti (-0.55), Seraikela (-0.69), Deoghar (-0.98), Dumka (-1.25), Pakaur (-0.89), Godda (-0.68) and Rajmahal (-0.59). Only one subdivision of Jamtara (-1.51) is characterised by very low level of development in housing and environment.

Spatial pattern of disparity in terms of the indicators of educational development has been depicted in the table. It is clear that educational development is very high in Godda (2.62), Dhanbad (2.16), Baghmara (1.90), Ranchi (1.66), Gumla (1.53) and Simdega (2.20).

A high level of educational development may be observed in four subdivisions, namely. Latehar (0.90), Dalbhum (113), Khunti (0.58) and Dumka (0.66).

Nearly half of the area comes under the category of medium level of educational development which is found in the north-western, southern, central and eastern part of the study area. The north-western region comprises Garhwa (-0.08), Daltonganj (0.36), Chatra (-0.22) and Lohardaga (-0.25). The southern region represents Chaibasa (-0.22) and Seraikela (-0.40). The central region consists of Bermo (-0.37), Giridih (-0.49) and Deoghar (-0.45) while the eastern region includes Pakaur (-0.21) and Rajmahal (-0.13).

There is only one region of low level of educational development located in the central part of the study area which includes the subdivision of Hazaribagh (-1.26) and Kodarma (0.61). Only one subdivision, Jamtara, records very low educational development.

Regional disparity as regards urbanisation shows that most of the highly urbanised areas are concentrated in the eastern and southern portion of the study area. The subdivisions recording a very high level of urbanisation are Dhanbad (2.61), Ranchi (1.63) and Dalbhum (2.13). A high level of urbanisation is found in only three subdivisions namely Bermo (0.80), Giridih (0.86) and Ranchi (1.41).

The areas of moderate urbanisation also occur in the eastern and southerns part adjacent to the areas of high urbanisation. They include Rajmahal (-0.38), Deoghar (-0.23), Chaibasa (-0.04), Seraikela (-0.23), Hazaribagh (0.33) and Lohandaga (-0.38).

The level of urbanisation is low in Jamtara (-0.77), Dumka (-0.68), Pakaur (-0.73) and Godda (-0.87). There is a large region of low level of urbanisation located in the western part of the study area comprising the subdivisions of Kodarma (0.51), Chatra (-0.70), Daltonganj (-0.54), Garhwa (-0.79), Latehar (-0.75), Gumla (-0.79), Simdega (-0.72) and Khunti (0.64).

Regional disparity in terms of security reveals that Dhanbad (2.06), and Chaibasa (1.65) are in a much better position.

Ranchi (1.27), Kunti (0.71), Seraikela (1.11), Dalbhum (1.41) and Baghmara (0.85) have been found in the grade of high security.

Three regions of medium security can be seen. One consists of the subdivisions of Simdega (0.09) and Gumla (0.27) located in the south-western part while the other comprises Garhwa (-0.14) and Daltonganj (0.19) in the north-west. The third region of medium security consists of Hazaribagh (-0.01), Giridih (-0.24), Deoghar (0.24) and Pakaur (-0.05).

There are two distinct regions of low security. One comprises Lohardaga (-0.93), Latehar (-0.78):, Chatra (-1.19), Kodarma (-1.07) and Bermo (-1.31) while the other region consists of Jamtara (-1.46), Dumka (-0.64), Godda (-1.40) and Rajmahal (-0.62).

Spatial pattern of disparity in terms of a group of indicators of occupational status reveals that the occupational status is very high in Dhanbad (1.82) subdivision. Six subdivisions, namely, Dalbhum (1.07), Chaibasa (0.64), Ranchi (1.02), Hazaribagh (0.55), Baghmara (1.18) and Pakaur (0.77) have been found in the category of high occupational status.

Most of the western and northern parts of the study area record medium occupational status which include the subdivisions of Simdega (0.00), Gumla (0.20), Seraikela (0.46), Khunti (0.18), Lohardaga (0.25), Latehar (0.33), Garhwa (-0.33), Daltonganj (-0.17), Chatra (-0.42), Kodarma (-0.35) and Giridih (-0.50). There are also two subdivisions, namely, Dumka (0.16) and Rajmahal (0.17) experiencing medium occupational status which are located in the north-eastern part.

The occupational status is low in Bermo (-0.84) and Jamtara (-1.26) whereas it is very low in Deoghar(-2.55) and Godda (-2.38).

Table 7 exhibits spatial pattern of size of lard-holdings. It clearly reveals that there are two small regions recording very large size of land holding in the central and eastern part which include Ranchi (1.94), Goda (1.60) and Rajmahal (2.12).

Most of the areas experiencing the large size of land holdings are confined to the central-west, south-east, and eastern part. They represent Lohardaga (0.79), Giridih (1.18), Dalbhum (1.05) and Pakaur (1.25).

Two regions of medium size of land holding can be observed. One is located in the extreme south comprising Chaibasa (-0.37) and Seraikela (0.34) while the other occurs in the central-eastern part and includes Hazaribagh (-0.24), Kodarma (00), Bermo (0.23), Baghmara (0.18), Dhanbad (0.03), Deoghar (-0.05) and Dumka (-0.32).

Most of the areas having very small and small size of land holdings lie in the western and north-western parts, except a small area in Jamtara. The areas of small size of land holdings comprise Simdega (-1.46) Gumla (-1.30). Khunti (-0.47), Garhwa (-1.16), Daltonganj (-1.44) and Chatra (-0.85). Latehar records very small size of land holdings (-1.54).

Table 7 throws light on regional disparity as regards agricultural development. The level of agricultural development is very high in two subdivisions, namely, Godda (1.55) and Pakaur (1.67).

The areas recording a high level of agricultural development are concentrated in the central and eastern parts. They include Simdega (0.60), Khunti (0.99), Seraikela (0.63), Lohardaga (0.81), Ranchi (0.99), Deoghar (0.96) and Dumka (0.87).

There are three isolated regions having a medium level of agricultural development which are located in the south-western, central-eastern and eastern parts. They comprise Chaibasa (0.11), Gumla (0.34), Baghmara (-0.42), Dhanbad (0.28), Jamtara (0.40) and Rajmahal (0.49).

The areas recording low and very low levels of agricultural development are found in the north-western half of the study area. There is a large compact region of low agricultural development which comprise the subdivisions of Garhwa (0.98), Latehar (-1.33), Daltonganj (-0.79), Hazaribagh (-1.05), Kodarma (-1.43), Giridih (-0.62), and Bermo (-1.24). There is also a small pocket of low level of agricultural development in Dalbhum (-0.89) which is detached from the main region.

Amid the large region of low level of agricultural development lies a single subdivision of Chatra having very low level (-1.71) of agricultural development.

The regional pattern of disparity in industrial development. It shows that the subdivisions of Dhanbad (3.54), Baghmara (2.34), Ranchi (2.03), Khunti (2.22), and Dalbhum (2.47) are highly developed in terms of industrialisation. Only one subdivision of Seraikela (1.03) records high level of industrial development.

The medium level of industrial development is found in the major parts of the study area which includes the subdivisions of Chaibasa (0.40), Simdega (-0.04), Gumla (-0.27; Lohardaga (0.38), Latehar (-0.42), Hazaribagh (-0.44), Kodarma (-0.48), Giridih (-0,43) and Pakaur (-0.42).

Most of the north-western and north-eastern parts experience a low level of industrial development. The former region comprises the subdivisions of Garhwa (-0.63), Daltonganj

(-0.61) and Chatra (-0.55)3 while the latter region consists of Deoghar (-0.66), Godda (-0.63), Rajmahal (-0.53), Dumka (-0.63), Jamtara (-0.63), and Bermo (0.52).

The regional pattern of social and economic disparities have been shown in Figure 3. A deep insight of the table reveals that there is a marked regional disparities in terms of overall socio-economic development in Chotanagpur plateau. Nearly one-fourth of the study area is highly developed which is confined to the south-eastern part and comprises the subdivisions of Dhanbad (2.04), Baghmara (1.63), Ranchi (1.68), Chaibasa (0.70) Seraikela (1.49) and Dalbhum (1.65).

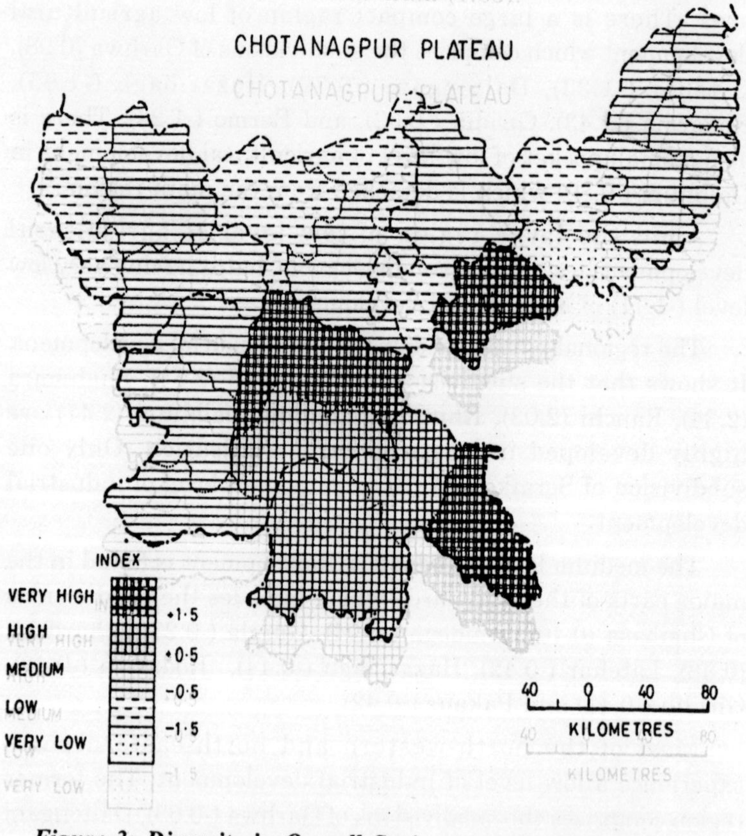

Figure 3: Disparity in Overall Socio-economic Development

Table 7

Socio-Economic Indicators: Standard Z-scores on Nine Critaria of Social and Economic Disparities

Sub-divisions	*Health Facilities*	*Hous-ing & Evniron.*	*Educat-ional Develop.*	*Urbani-sation*	*Security*	*Occupat-ional Status*	*Size of Land-Holding*	*Level of Agri. Develop.*	*Level of Industiral Develop.*	*Overall Socio-economic develop.*
1. Dumka	0.00	-1.25	0.66	-0.68	-0.64	0.16	-0.32	0.87	-0.63	-0.41
2. Jamtara	-2.55	-1.51	-1.60	-0.77	-1.46	-1.26	-1.12	0.40	-0.63	-2.35
3. Deoghar	-1.54	-0.98	-0.45	-0.23	0.24	-2.55	-0.05	0.96	-0.66	-1.17
4. Godda	-0.16	-0.68	2.62	-0.87	-1.40	-2.38	1.60	1.55	-0.63	-0.19
5. Rajmahal	-1.25	-0.59	-0.13	-0.38	-0.62	0.17	2.12	0.49	-0.53	-0.16
6. Fakaur	0.14	-0.59	-0.21	-0.73	-0.05	0.77	1.25	1.67	-0.42	0.34
7. Dhanbad	-0.26	0.79	2.16	2.61	2.06	1.82	0.03	-0.28	3.54	2.04
8. Baghmara	1.00	1.66	1.90	1.41	0.85	1.18	0.18	-0.42	2.34	1.63
9. Giridih	-0.15	-0.17	-0.49	0.86	-0.24	-0.50	0.64	-0.62	-0.43	-0.24
10. Bermo	-1.40	0.03	-0.37	0.80	-1.31	-0.84	0.23	-1.24	-0.52	-1.03
11. Hazaribagh	0.44	0.83	-1.26	0.33	-0.01	0.55	-0.24	-1.05	-0.44	-0.19
12. Chatra	1.10	0.62	-0.22	-0.70	-1.19	-0.42	-0.85	-1.71	-0.55	-0.87
13. Kodarma	0.28	0.29	-0.61	-0.51	-1.07	-0.35	0.00	-1.43	-0.48	-0.86
14. Daltonganj	-0.07	1.93	0.36	-0.54	0.19	-0.17	-0.57	-0.79	-0.61	-0.06
15. Latehar	2.55	0.12	0.97	-0/75	-0.78	0.33	-1.54	-1.33	-0.42	-0.19
16. Garhwa	-0.04	0.17	-0.08	-0.79	-0.14	0.33	-1.16	-0.98	-0.63	-0.89
17. Ranchi	0.12	0.93	1.66	1.63	1.27	1.02	1.94	1.32	2.03	1.68
18. Khunti	-0.62	-0.55	0.58	-0.64	0.71	0.18	-0.47	8.99	2.22	0.05
19. Simdega	0.38	-1.06	2.20	-0.72	0.09	0.00	-1.46	0.60	-0.04	0.00
20. Gumla	0.71	-1.20	1.53	-0.79	0.27	0.20	-1.30	0.34	-0.27	-0.11
21. Lohardaga	1.10	0.48	-0.25	-0.28	-0.93	0.25	0.79	0.81	0.38	0.29
22. Chaibasa	0.39	0.60	-0.22	-0.04	1.65	0.64	-0.37	0.11	0.40	0.70
23. Seraibela	-0.06	-0.69	-0.40	-0.23	1.11	0.46	0.34	0.63	1.03	1.49
24. Dalbhum	-0.09	2.09	1.13	2.13	1.41	1.07	1.05	-0.89	2.47	1.65

Nearly 50 per cent of the study area records a medium level of social and economic development which lies in the central-western as well as the north-eastern part. It comprises the sub-divisions of Giridih (-0.24), Gumla (-0.11), Lohardaga (0.29), Latehar (-0.19), Daltonganj (-0.06), Simdega (0.00) Hazaribagh (-0.19), Dumka (-0.41), Godda (-0.19), Rajmahal (-0.16) and Pakaur (0.34). Very high or a high level of socio-economic development of this region may be attributed to their high degree of industrialisation and urbanisation. The location of industries in this region has been encouraged by the occurrence of a variety of minerals, and availability of industrial infrastructure. It has dense transport network and is also connected with the territories outside the study area such as Kolkata and Mumbai and has attracted entrepreneurs from outside. A maximum number of urban centres are also located in this area which also provide industries with infrastructure.

The high level of social and economic development of this region is also contributed by the concentration of other facilities such as health, education, housing and environment and security.

The areas recording a low level of social and economic development are found in the north-western part consisting of the subdivision of Deoghar (-1.17), Kodarma (-0.86), Chatra (0.87) and Garhwa (-0.89). Only one subdivision, Jamtara, records a very low level of social and economic development. Inaccessibility by roads and railways appears to be the main hindrance for the growth of industries and urban centres.

5

Factorial Analysis of Social and Economic Disparities

In the previous chapter, the regional pattern of disparities in terms of nine sets of socio-economic indicators and their composite index have been measured. However their causes are not empirically examined. Therefore, it would be worthwhile to study various dimensions of inequalities and analyse factors responsible for their creation. Such an attempt has been made in this chapter using the technique of Factor Analysis. The Factor Analysis conducted for this study is based on 20 variables pertaining to social and economic disparities as reflected in the social, economic, demographic and production characteristics of the population of 24 subdivisions of the Chotanagpur plateau.

Data analysis was carried on VAX-11 computing system. The programme of the Factor Analysis is available in the stored standard subroutine package which gives a principal component solution.

FACTOR STRUCTURE

The factor analysis of 20 variables related to the social and economic characteristics has yielded five factors (Table 8) which together account for 77.73 per cent of the total variance in the spatial dimension of social and economic disparities. An examination of the rotated factor loadings on these factors rendered them to be labelled as urbanisation and socio-economic development, institutional factors and agricultures under development, work participation and infrastructural stress, educational development and miscellaneous factors. As regards the contribution of these factors, urbanisation and socio-economic development explains 25.94 per cent of the total variance, institutional factors and agriculture under development 14.17 per cent, work participation and infrastructural stress 13.42 per cent, educational development 12.55 per cent and miscellaneous factors.

Table 8

Dimensions of Social and Economic Disparities in Chotanagpur

1.	Urbanisation and socio-economic development	25.94%
2.	Institutional factor and agriculture under development	14.17%
3.	Work participation and infrastructural stress	13.42%
4.	Educational status	12,55%
5.	Miscellaneous factors	11,71%
	Percentage of total variance explained by five factors	77.79%

FACTOR I : URBANISATION AND SOCIO-ECONOMIC DEVELOPMENT

The first factor accounts for 25.94 per cent of the total variance of social and economic disparities and closely identified with urbanisation and socio-economic development. The nature of the factor is defined by very high loadings for beds per lakh of population (0.89792), doctors per lakh of population (0.89173), percentage of pucca houses to the total houses (0.66135), percentage urban population to the total population (0.68519), number of police per lakh of population (0.77943), percentage of non-agricultural workers to the total population (0.70492) and number of registered working factories per 10,000 of population (0.75537).

A deep insight of the relationships of loadings of the first factor indicates that urbanisation which is defined in terms of the proportion of population engaged in non-agricultural activities determines the social and economic development of Chotanagpur plateau. In this analysis it has been observed that almost all indicators of social and economic development are positively associated with urbanisation. It means that rural areas and rural population of the study area are much backward socially and economically as compared to their urban counterpart. Myint[1] has rightly stated that industrialisation is popularly regarded as synonymous with the economic development by the people of developing countries. He feels that agriculture is an inherently less productive occupation than manufacturing, and that the present economic structure of those countries which are characterised by a large proportion of total working force in primary production is somehow lopsided and unbalanced, and should be cared by an overall drive for manufacturing industries. He further points out that it is not unfair to say that the bias in favour of industrialisation seems to be shared even by economists who advocate the 'balance growth' approach only within the manufacturing sectors. This bias for manufacturing seems to arise partly out of the feeling that before the developing countries can proceed along the balance growth path, the initial imbalance between their agriculture and manufacturing industries must be cured by starting with counterbalancing of manufacturing industries.

The very high positive loading for police per lakh population (0.71900) suggests that urban centres are more prone to crime, therefore, adequate number of police are kept to maintain law and order. It is an observed fact that urban areas have better reinforcement of police service. Although statistics on crime all over the world confirms the urban bias and it does not require geographical boundaries, yet it has been widely accepted that rural areas are more idyllic. However, it should be noted that rural areas are not free from crimes, rather it is under reporting of crimes and slack police service in rural areas as a result of which criminals are less likely to be brought into the national system of justice.

Table 9

Factor I : Urbanisation and Socio-Economic Development

Indicators	*Factor Loadings*
1. Hospitals/100,000 of Population	–0.00750
2. Public health centres/10,000 of population	–0.27223
3. Beds/100,000 of population	0.89792
4. Doctors/100,000 of population	0.89173
5. Percentage of pucca houses/total houses	0.66135
6. Percentage of houseless/total population	0.08203
7. Drinking water	–0.02537
8. Percentage of electrified villages/total villages	0.48507
9. Percentage of literates/total population	0.48565
10. Primary schools/100,000 of population	–0.55686
11. Middle schools/100,000 of population	–0.20857
12. Secondary schools/100,00 of population	– 0.08257
13. Percentage of urban population total population	– 0.68519
14. Police/100,000 of population	0.77943
15. Percentage of main worker/total population	0.00921
16. Percentage of non agricultural workers/ total population	0.70492
17. Percentage of small and marginal land holdings/total holding	0.00469
18. Percentage of net sown area & total area	0.04342
19. Agricultural productivity per hectare (in Rs.)	0.07326
20. Factories/10,000 of population	0.75537
Per cent of variance explained	25.94%

The very high loadings for beds per lakh of population (0.89792) and doctors per lakh of population (0.89173) are indication that the highly urbanised areas of Chotanagpur are well served with medical care facilities. The negative loadings of hospital and public health centres with this factor explain the fact that though in urban areas the number of hospitals and dispensaries are comparatively less than the rural areas yet they are big and have a large number of beds and doctors.

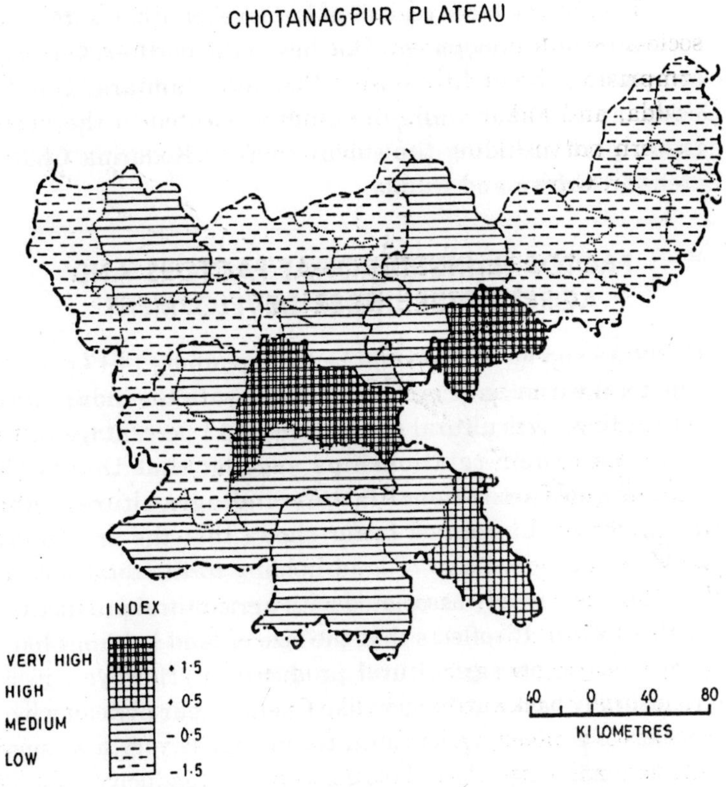

Figure 4

Urbanisation and Socio-economic Development (Factor-I)

Figure 4 shows spatial pattern of urbanisation and socio-economic development. It reveals that the areas of very high factor scores of urbanisation and socio-economic development are confined to three subdivisions, namely, Dhanbad, Baghmara and Ranchi. There is only one subdivision, Dalbhum, recording high urbanisation.

The major part of Chotanagpur plateau comes under the category of medium level of urbanisation and socio-economic development which includes Giridih, Bermo, Hazaribagh, Daltonganj, Lohardaga, Simdega, Chaibasa, Khunti and Seraikela.

There are two large regions of low level of urbanisation and socio-economic development. One lies in the north-eastern part comprising the subdivisions of Deoghar, Jamtara, Dumka, Godda, and Pakaur while the other is located in the north-eastern part including the subdivisions of Kodarma Chatra, Latehar, Garhwa and Gumla.

FACTOR II: INSTITUTIONAL FACTORS AND AGRICULTURE UNDER DEVELOPMENT

This the second most important factor explaining 14.17 per cent of the total variance. It is closely related with the indicators of land holding, agricultural productivity and percentage of net sown area. Their relationships suggest that this is the dimension of institutional factors and agriculture, under development. The rotated factor shows that the area under small and marginal size of land holding to the total holding (0.95324) is positively associated with agricultural productivity in Rs (0.45840). It reflects that the size of land holdings has a direct bearing on agricultural productivity. However, in an agriculturally backward region like Chotanagpur plateau where adoption of modern agricultural technology is very low, small and marginal size of land holdings are not conducive for high agricultural productivity. It is mainly due to the fact that small and marginal farmers are very poor who cannot afford to use adequate amount of agricultural inputs in their fields which is very essential for high yield. Though these farmers devote much of their time in farm practices, yet their manual labour without sufficient use of fertilisers, high yielding varieties of seeds, insecticides and pesticides, and agricultural machines proves less effective. Many of the small and marginal farmers who tried to adopt the high yielding varieties of rice and wheat without essential complementary inputs could not perform well and many of them have, therefore, retreated to old subsistence farming or have taken advantage of rising land prices to sell out their lands to clear their debts and have attempted a new start in life.[2]

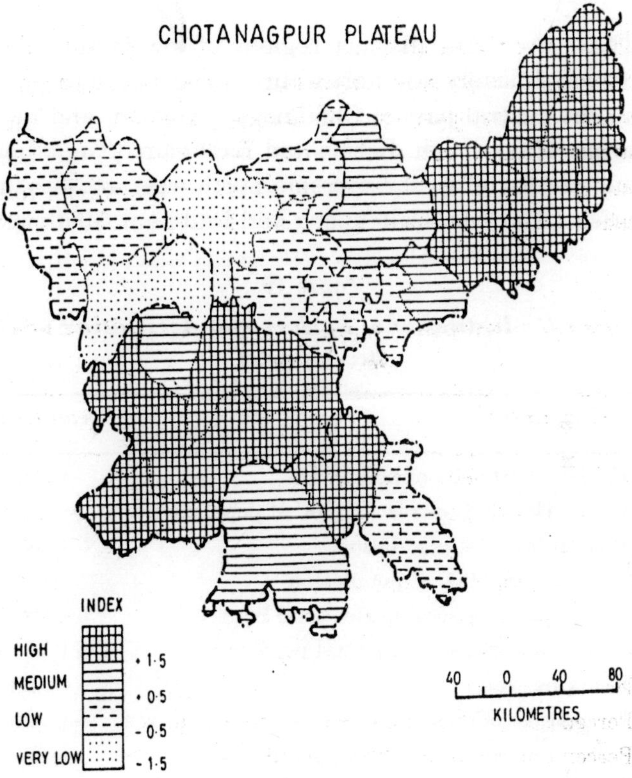

Figure 5

Institutional Factor and Agricultural Underdevelopment (Factor-II)

The spatial pattern of institutional factors and agricultures under development has been portrayed in Figure 5. It is clear from the map that most of the subdivisions lying in the north-eastern and southern part record high factor scores for institutional factors and agriculture under development. The regions of high factor score comprise Rajmahal, Godda, Pakaur, Dumka, Deoghar, Jamtara, Ranchi, Gumla, Simdega, Khunti and Seraikela.

The subdivisions recording medium factor score are Giridih, Dhanbad, Lohardega and Chaibasa.

There are three distinct regions of low factor scores of institutional factors and agriculture under development. One lies in the central part of Chotanagpur plateau and includes Kodarma, Haxaribagh, Bermo and Baghmara. The other two regions are found in the extreme north-west and south-east comprising Garhwa, Daltongang and Dalbhum subdivisions.

Table 10

Factor II : Institutional Factors and Agriculture under Development

	Indicators	*Factor Loadings*
1.	Hospitals/100,000 of population	–0.32102
2.	Public Health Centres/100,000 of population	–0.08260
3.	Beds/100,000 of population	0.06113
4.	Doctors/1,000,000 of population	0.04833
5.	Percentage of pucca houses/total houses	– 0.22290
6.	Percentage of houseless/total population	– 0.38804
7.	Drinking water	–0.50360
8.	Percentage of electrified villages/ total villages	–0.32946
9.	Percentage of literates/total population	0.09956
10.	Primary schools/100,000 of population	0.24604
11.	Middle schools/100,000 of population	0.09802
12.	Secondary schools/100,000 population	0.09527
13.	Percentage of urban population/total population	– 0.10332
14.	Police/100,000 of population	0.15994
15.	Percentage of main workers/total population	– 0.00921
16.	Percentage of non-agricultural workers/total population	0.00142
17.	Percentage of small and marginal land holdings/total holdings	0.95324
18.	Percentage of net-sown area/total area	0.44978
19.	Agricultural productivity per hectare (in Rs.)	0.45840
20.	Factories/10,000 of population	0.04219
	Per cent of variance explained	14.17%

Chatra and Latehar subdivisions have very low factor scores.

FACTOR III : WORK PARTICIPATION AND INFRASTRUCTURAL STRESS

The third factor explains 13.42 per cent of the total variance of social and economic disparities and labelled as work participation and infrastructural stress. This factor is composed of five variables, namely, the percentage of main workers to the total population, hospitals per lakh of population, primary health centres per lakh of population, and middle schools per lakh of population. The high positive loadings for the percentage of main workers to the total population (0.67455) has its negative association with hospitals (-0.80025), primary health centres (-0.85413), primary schools (-0. 41422) and middle schools (-0.56633). The relationships of these variables reflect the rural character of this factor because in rural areas the work participation rate is comparatively higher than urban centres but infrastructural facilities such as hospitals and schools are lacking. During the last few decades, the number of schools in rural areas of Chotanagpur has increased but it is neither in proportion to its rapidly increasing population nor uniformly distributed over space. Most of the primary and secondary schools are concentrated in urban areas while the rural areas have been neglected. So the middle and secondary school-going children have to cover a long distance from their homes to schools which consume much of their time and energy and adversely affect their educational attainment. This problem, especially in tribal areas, is further aggravated by the establishment of single-teacher school, deficiencies in school building and equipment, recruitment of teachers unequianted with tribal language and culture and their weak motivation and unwillingness to stay in tribal areas.

The negative loadings on primary health centres and hospitals is an indication of poor medical facilities available to the people. In a report on rural health services, Banerji[3] points out that the common image of the dispensary found in villages is far from favourable. "Complaints about medicine and overcrowding and long waiting are made against the best of public health centres studied." But the difficulty is not only the sheer number of patients, they seem as much to be due to deficiencies in personnel and to the cultural gap between patients and health workers. The local health workers and auxiliary nurses, midwives are seen as "meant for special people or those who can pay for their services." Lady doctors are seen as even more inaccessible. The research findings as reported by Banerji show that workers of rural health and other development agencies generally have a strong distaste for rural life. The distaste is for the entire way of life and not simply for very poor facilities available there. Hence, they keep their distance from the rural folk among whom they work. The apparently common characteristic naturally limits the effectiveness of health centres as an institution. Thus, it can be stated that making quantitative additions to the health services or giving "orientation training" will not remedy this deep-seated malady, which requires sweeping changes and the culture of bureaucracy.

Table 11

Factor III : Work Participation and Infrastructural Stress

Indicators	*Factor Loadings*
1. Hospitals/100,000 of population	–0.80025
2. Public health centres/100,000 of population	–0.85413
3. Beds/100,000 of population	0.10596
4. Doctors/100,000 of population	0.09879
5. Percentage of pucca houses/total houses	0.24621
6. Percentage of houseless/total population	–0.12504
7. Drinking water	–0.35370
8. Percentage of electrified villages/total villages	0.12157
9. Percentage of literates/total population	0.04143
10. Primary schools/100,000 of population	–0.41422
11. Middle schools/100,000 of population	–0.56633
12. Secondary schools/100,000 of population	–0.08232

(Contd...)

13.	Percentage of urban population/total population	0.23437
14.	Police/100,000 of population	–0.12797
15.	Percentage of main workers/total population	0.67455
16.	Percentage of non-agricultural workers/ total population	–0.06881
17.	Percentage, of small and marginal land holding/ total holdings	0.08385
18.	Percentage of net sown area/total area	0.15784
19.	Agricultural productivity per hectare (in Rs)	0.07912
20.	Factories/100,00 of population	0.08267
	Per cent of variance explained	13.42%

Figure 6 shows spatial pattern of work participation and infrastructural stress. A cursory glance of the map reveals that about 45 per cent of the area records a high factor score for work participation and infrastructural stress. The subdivisions recording high factor scores are Rajmahal, Godda, Pakaur, Deoghar, Dumka, Ranchi, Gumla, Simdega, Khunti and Seraikela.

Medium factor scores may be observed in Giridih, Dhanbad, Chaibasa and Lohardaga.

The areas of low factor scores for work participation and infrastructural stress are spread in different parts which include Garhwa and Daltonganj in the west, Kodarma, Hazaribagh, Bermo and Baghmara in the centre and Dalbhum in the south.

Only Chatra and Latehar have very low factor scores for this dimension and they are located in the eastern part of the study area.

FACTOR IV: EDUCATIONAL STATUS

The fourth factor accounts for 12.55 per cent of the total variance of social and economic disparities and may be called

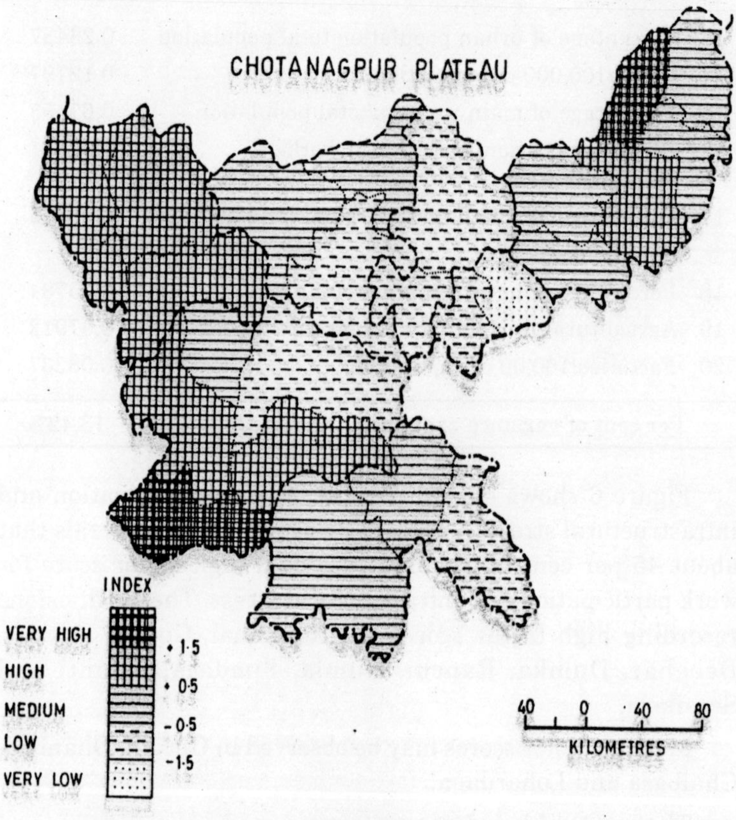

Figure 6

Work Participation and Infrastructural Stress (Factor-III)

educational status. This factor has very high positive loadings for secondary schools per lakh of population (0.86785), middle schools per lakh of population (0.69529) and moderate positive loading for primary schools per lakh of population (0.43007). But the relation of these variables with percentage of literates to the total population is very weak (0.26145) which indicates that in spite of concentration of schools in Chotanagpur plateau, the majority of its population remains illiterate and uneducated. It is because the major part of this region has tribal concentration. Though the government has opened many schools in order to educate and improve the socio-econmic conditions of tribals, yet they have not been fully benefited by the educational facilities due to their poor economic conditions, superstitions, boring curriculum and unsuitable teachers.

Table 12

Factor IV : Educational Status

	Indicators	*Factor Loadings*
1.	Hospitals/100,000 of population	0.17585
2.	Public health centres/100,000 of population	0.21327
3.	Beds/10,000 of population	0.02559
4.	Doctors/100,000 of population	0.03862
5.	Percentage of pucca houses/total houses	–0.38533
6.	Percentage of houseless/total population	–0.34777
7.	Drinking water	0.3 3808
8.	Percentage of electrified villages/total villages	0.15788
9.	Percentage of literates/total population	0.26145
10.	Primary schools/100,000 of population	0.43007
11.	Middle schools/100,000 of population	0.69529
12.	Secondary schools/100,000 of population	0.86785
13.	Percentage of urban population/total population	–0.38764
14.	Police/100,000 of population	–0.10502
15.	Percentage of main workers/total population	–0.25726
16.	Percentage of non-agricultural workers/ total population	–0.34338
17.	Percentage of small and marginal land holding/total holdings	0.20037
18.	Percentage of net sown area/total area	–0.25877
19.	Agricultural productivity per hectare (in Rs.)	0.17410
20.	Factories/10,000 of population	–0.22697
	Per cent of variance explained	12.55%

The most important factor which hinders the growth of tribal education is their extreme poverty. Most of the tribals earn their livelihood either by hunting, food gathering, fishing or agriculture which are of subsistence nature and do not provide sufficient food for the requirement of their family. In such conditions education is an item of least importance to them. In tribal families each child is an earning member. If he goes to school his parents not only lose the income which he contributes but also bear additional economic burden on his education. Also the present education system in our country is such that a child is not able to earn economic benefit for his family before 15 or 20 years which is required for his education. The tribal parents have no patience to wait for such a long period. That is why they discourage education for their children.

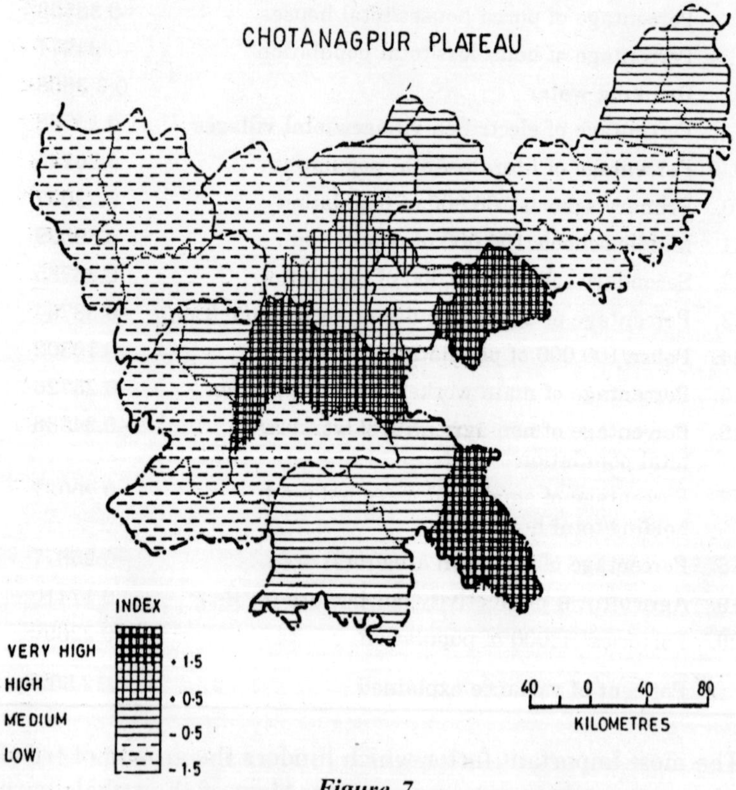

Figure 7

Educational Status (Factor-IV)

Except for a few advanced tribes such as the Santhals, the Oraon, the Ho and the Munda, still there is widespread feeling in most of the tribes that education makes their boys disobedient and contemptuous and alienate them from the rest of the society, while girls turn modern or become westernised, Some of the students, after education and good jobs get cut off from their societies and villages. Therefore, parents oppose their formal education. It is also handicapped by superstitions and myths prevalent among tribals. They believe that God will be angry, if they send their children to schools run by outsiders.

The spatial variations of factor IV is depicted on Figure 7 which indicates that Dhanbad, Baghmara, Ranchi and Dalbhum subdivisions record very high factor scores for educational status, while only one subdivision, namely, Hazaribagh, comes under the category of high factor scores.

Medium factor scores for educational status are observed in Rajmahal, Godda, pakaur, Kodarma, Giridih, Bermo, Lohardaga, Chaibasa and Śeraikela which form four isolated regions.

Three regions of low factor scores may be observed, one lies in the north-eastern part while the remaining two in the north-western and south-eastern part of the study area.

FACTOR V: MISCELLANEOUS

This factor explains 11.7 per cent of the total variance and is composed of the diversified nature of variables. It is, therefore, difficult to give it any satisfactory nomenclature and has been named as miscellaneous factor. The highest positive loadings have been recorded for percentage of literates to the total population (0.72976), percentage of houseless to the total population (0.65566), percentage of net sown area to the total area (0.62606) and moderate positive loading for percentage of pucca houses to the total houses (0.41331), percentage of urban population to the total population (0.48739) and percentage of non-agricultural workers to the total population (0.48545).

The regional pattern of miscellaneous factor has been shown in Figure 8. It reveals that Bermo and Jamtara record a very high score for this factor. Both these subdivisions lie in the eastern part but do not form a compact block.

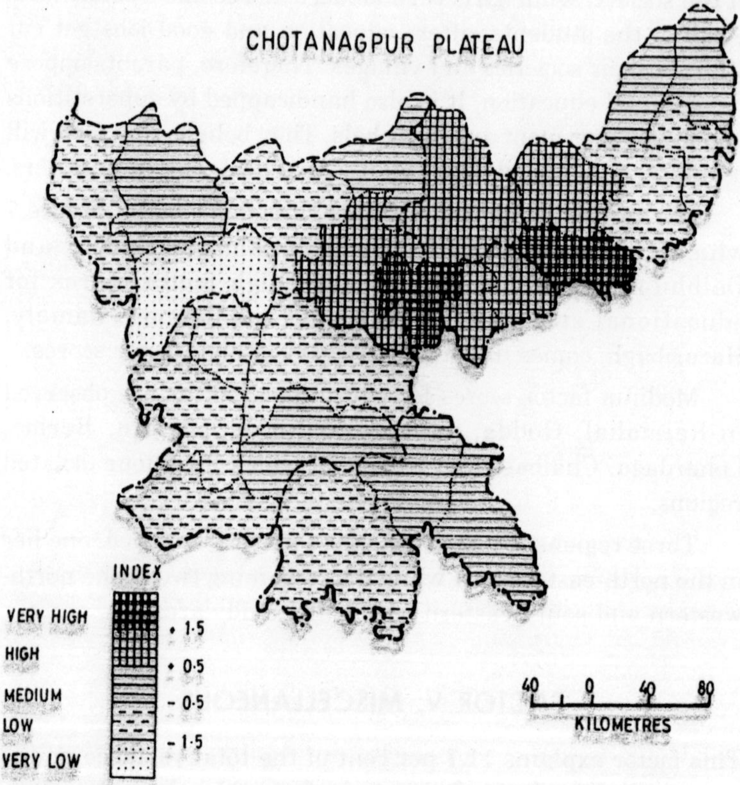

Figure 8

Miscellaneous Factor (Factor-V)

There is a large compact region of high factor scores located in the central part of the study area. It includes the subdivisions of Hazaribagh, Giridih, Dhanbad, Deoghar and Jamtara.

The subdivisions having medium factor scores are scattered over different parts of the study area. They include Godda,

Rajmahal, Koderma, Daltonganj, Khunti, Seraikela and Dalbhum.

The majority of the subdivisions come under the category of low factor scores for this dimension and constitute two separate regions. One of them lies in the western part comprising Garhwa, Lohardaga, Gumla, Simdega, Ranchi and Chaibasa. The other region of low factor scores comprises Pakaur and Dumka. Only one subdivision, Latehar, comes under the very low category.

Table 13

Factor V: Miscellaneous Factors

Indicators	*Factor Loadings*
1. Hospitals/100,000 of population	0.10278
2. Public health centres/100,000 of population	0.04792
3. Beds/100,000 of population	0.00001
4. Doctors/100,000 of population	-0.02645
5. Percentage of pucca houses/total houses	0.41331
6. Percentage of houseless/total population	0.65566
7. Drinking water	0.03607
8. Percentage of electrified villages/total villages	-0.10418
9. Percentage of literates/total population	0.72976
10. Primary schools/100,000 of population	-0.24209
11. Middle schools/100,000 of population	-0.22974
12. Secondary schools/100,000 of population	-0.07199
13. Percentage of urban population/total population	0.48739
14. Police/100,000 of population	0.10929
15. Percentage of main workers/total population	-0.36419
16. Percentage of non-agricultural workers/ total population.	0.48545
17. Percentage of small and marginal land holding/total holdings	0.00859
18. Percentage of net sown area/total area	0.62606
19. Agricultural productivity per hectare (in Rs .)	-0.00590
20. Factories/10,000 of population	0.24197
Per cent of variance explained	11.7%

Table 14

Standarised Scores of Social and Economic Disparities

	Factor I	*Factor II*	*Factor III*	*Factor IV*	*Factor V*
1. Dumka	-0.97	0.91	0.62	-0.91	-0.70
2. Jamtara	-0.88	0.55	-0.41	-0.85	1.66
3. Deoghar	-0.85	1.09	0.35	-0.67	1.20
4. Godda	-1.01	1.48	1.93	0.39	0.07
5. Rajmahal	-0.60	0.80	0.04	-0.08	0.39
6. Pakaur	-0.76	1.48	0.10	-0.37	-0.71
7. Dhanbad	2.71	-0.09	-1.94	2.02	1.36
8. Baghmara	1:96	-0.78	-1.31	1.66	0.68
9. Giridih	0.25	-0.14	-0.56	0.16	0.67
10. Bermo	0.04	-0.83	-1.24	0.29	1.52
11. Hazaribagh	0.41	-1.00	-1.22	0.66	0.78
12. Chatra	-0.85	-1.75	0.21	-0.57	-1.19
13. Kodarma	-0.69	-1.27	-0.25	0.08	-0.32
14. Daltonganj	0.04	-1,13	0.91	-0.72	-0.37
15. Latehar	-0.85	-1.54	1.23	1.02	-2.49
16. Garhwa	-0.74	-1.06	0.65	-1.04	-0.81
17. Ranchi	1.99	1.08	-1.05	+1.53	1.38
18. Khunti	0.23	1.07	0.54	-9.78	-0.01
19. Simdega	-0,16	0.57	1.61	-1 .04	-0.68
20. Gumla	-0.57	0.78	1.36	-1.09	-1.12
21. Lohardaga	-0.11	0.14	-0.00	-0.03	-0.62
22. Chaibasa	0.22	-0.18	0.08	-0.17	-0.50
23. Seraikela	0.15	0.62	-0.19	0.11	-0.33
24. Dalbhum	1.06	-1.01	-1.41	2.47	0.13

REFERENCES

1. Myint, H., *The Economics of Developing Countries*, London, The Hutichinson Univ. Lib., 1967, p. 129.
2. Husain, M., Diffusion of High Yielding varieties of Rice and wheat in India and Social Tension, edited in Shaft M. and Aziz A., Ford Systems of the World, Rawat Publications, Jaipur, 1989, p. 56.
3. Banerji, D., Health Behaviour of Rural Population: Impact of Rural Health Services, *Economic and Political Weekly*, pp. 2264 and 2267.

6

Regional Patterns of Socio-economic Disparities between General Population and Scheduled Tribes

For a long time the Indian tribes have been a victim of economic exploitation and social discrimination. During the last 55 years, efforts have been made to alter the fate of tribal people living in different parts of India. However, the desired results have not been achieved and our objectives have been suffered. It is due to the loopholes in the strategies adopted for tribal development that we have failed to achieve the goals of improving the standard of living of tribes and to bring them into the national mainstream.

Tribals constitute an important segment of the population of Chotanagpur plateau. They account for about 30.25 per cent of the total population of the region. In spite of being aboriginal, tribals have not been fully benefited by the development of this region which is reflected in their very low socio-economic condition as compared to non-tribals. As we know, this region is very rich in mineral resources and is also comparatively developed in industrialisation and urbanisation but the fruits of development have largely been exploited by non-tribal outsiders because they are socially and culturally more advanced than tribal people. This has led to a wide gap in the level of living of tribal and non-tribal population which clearly reflects in their occupational status, literacy level, employment, wealth and income, and housing and health condition.

In the present chapter an attempt has been made to measure inequalities between tribal and non-tribal population of Chotanagpur plateau in terms of indicators such as literacy, proportion of urban population to the total population, percentage of non-agricultural workers to the total population, percentage of non-workers, and percentage of houseless population to the total population. The cross-inequality of these two ethnic groups has been quantified at the district level by using the techniques of Simple Differentials. The differentials of each selected indicator have been categorised by quartile method and have been shown on the map.

The differentials (disparities) of each selected indicators have been worked out by the following formula:

$$\frac{L_1 - L_2}{A} \times 100$$

where

L_1 stands for higher value of as indicator

L_2 stand for lower value of the same indicator

A stands for the relative average of L_1 and L_2

The importance of education for the overall development of tribals has been emphasised by time to time all the commissions. To equip the tribals to broaden their outlook and build up their, confidence it would be extremely useful to educate them. Table15 reveals that only 17.52 per cent of the total population of Chotanagpur population are literate, while literacy among non-tribals is 26.21 per cent. It clearly shows that tribals of this region are far behind in literacy than non-tribals and there is a literacy gap of 39.77 per cent between these two ethnic groups. The reasons for educational backwardness are numerous. The present student population of scheduled tribes is the first generation learners lack parental support and values of formal education. The majority of parents are illiterate, hence they show and lack keenness to send their children to schools on a regular and sustained manner.

Table 15

Socio-economic Disparities between Tribals and Non-tribals (Overall)

	Literacy %	*Non-agricultural Workers %*	*Urban Pop. %*	*Non-workers %*	*Houseless %*
Tribals	17.52	5.18	6.34	53.92	4.25
Non-tribals	26.72	9.80	26.35	62.73	2.83
Disparity	39.77	61.68	123.01	15.10	40.11

Also tribal children to a larger extent remain illiterate and uneducated due to economic reasons. They augment the workforce in their family and thus generate income for their parents. Therefore, the parents think that if their children are sent to school their work would suffer causing heavy loss. Such attitude of parents towards the education of their children is mainly due to their impoverished condition and poor economic standard of living. Although some tribal parents and guardians have realised the values of education, yet they are not in a position to wait for such a long time to let their children earn after completion of their formal education. In fact, the present system of education is neither favourable for the socio-economic development of the tribals nor any significant attempt has been made to integrate the system of education and socio-economic problems of the tribals.

There are some other educational impediments also. The dropout, rate particularly at the elementary stage among tribal students, is alarmingly high (77.9 %) in the study area. Though a large number of tribal children get enrolled in schools lured by scholarships and other financial assistance, yet they do not attend classes regularly, and frequently give up education.

Hence there is a need to educate and convince guardians regarding the benefits and necessities of the education of their children. Also the number of schools in tribal-dominated areas are less than non-tribal areas. Further, the medium of teaching and content of the courses are out of orientation and mental susceptibility and receptivity of the tribal students. The tribal students are taught about such things personalities about which they are ignorant. The medium of their instruction is the state language rather than their own dialect. Therefore they are not keenly interested in education.

As regards the participation of scheduled tribes and non-tribes in non-agricultural activities, it accounts for 5.18 per cent and 9.80 per cent respectively. There is disparity of 61.68 per cent in the share of non-agricultural workers between tribals and non-tribals the study area. This phenomena of under-representation of tribals in secondary and tertiary sectors may be explained by two factors. It is partly due to their educational backwardness and partly discrimination against them in appointment. The educational level of the majority of tribes is so low that it is incompatible with the requirements of industries, trade and transport. Even if some of them are trained and competent, there is a step motherly treatment against them in their appointment. Though government has provided reservation in jobs to scheduled tribes, yet their appointment is delayed and posts are kept vacant.

Urbanisation is an index of modernisation and economic development of any region or society. The social significance of urbanisation lies in the fact that first and foremost it reflects a change in the occupational pattern which in turn throws light on the income pattern, thus triggering the forces essential for the enhancement of material standard and higher social values of life. Its social significance is portrayed by better facilities provided in the forms of educational and medical institutions, banking facilities, etc., which result in wide disparities in the pattern of rural and urban living. In case of Chotanagpur plateau a large proportion of tribal population lives in rural areas. The percentage of tribals inhabiting urban areas is as low as nearly five times less than as compared to the non-tribals This figure clearly indicates that the position of tribal population in this respect is far from satisfactory. One of its reasons may be that since generation to generation their life and activities have been associated with forest and hill environment, therefore they are reluctant to go into a new urban environment.

As far as the percentage of non-workers of Chotanagpur is concerned, it is lower in the case of tribal population. The percentage of non-workers in tribals is 53.92 per cent while it is as high as 62.73 per cent in non-tribals. In this way there is disparity of 15.10 per cent in employment which is in favour of tribal people. The higher share of tribals in economically gainful activities is due to the fact that besides males, a considerable number of females and children are also engaged in economic activities. However, it does not mean that economically their position is very sound because most of them are engaged in primary activities which are less remunerative.

Housing is a basic need of society. Proper housing exercises profound influence on people's health and is recognised as an important indicator of the level of living. It is a matter of utmost importance in the social welfare programmes of all states. A poor houseless man would never be able to assert his right unless his possession over home is secure. Thus housing has become a part of struggle for economic emancipation, It is also essential for man to live in peace and dignity. Housing is very much related to work and interlinked with an overall socio-economic development.

Though the problem of houselessness is observed both in tribal and non-tribal population of the study area yet it is severe in tribals. A cursory glance of Table 15 the reveals that the percentage of houseless is 4.2 per cent among tribes as against 2.83 per cent among non-tribals. This disparity of houselessness between tribals and non-tribals reflects the fact that a large section of the tribal populations are so poor that the people are not able to possess their own houses.

The spatial pattern of literacy differentials between tribal and non-tribal population of Chotanagpur plateau has been shown in Figure 9. It reveals that there are three distinct regions of very high literacy differentials. One lies in the central part of the study area comprising Kodarma, Giridih, Dhanbad and Bermo. The other lies in Godda and Dalbhum subdivisions.

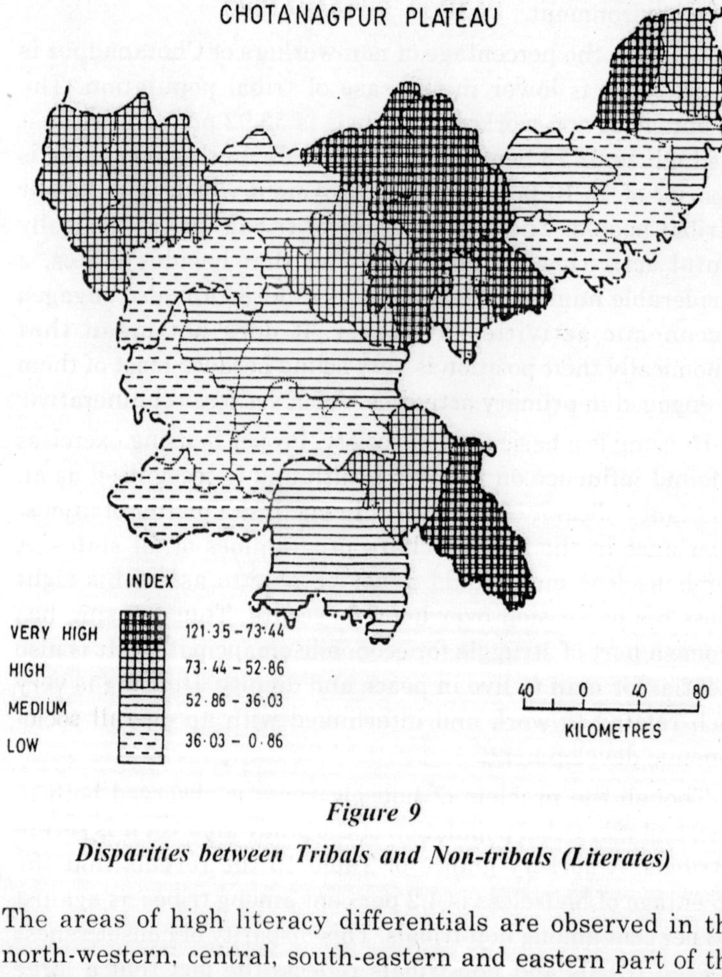

Figure 9

Disparities between Tribals and Non-tribals (Literates)

The areas of high literacy differentials are observed in the north-western, central, south-eastern and eastern part of the study area which includes Garhwa, Daltonganj, Hazaribagh, Seraikela and Rajmahal subdivisions.

The subdivisions recording medium literacy differentials comprise Chatra, Lohardaga, Ranchi, Chaibasa, Deoghar and Pakaur. Among them Chatra, Ranchi and Lohardaga form a compact region and rest of the subdivisions of medium literacy differentials are found scattered.

Two regions of low literacy differentials may be noticed which are found in the central-western and the north-eastern parts which include Latehar, Gumla, Simdega, Khunti, Dumka and Jamtara.

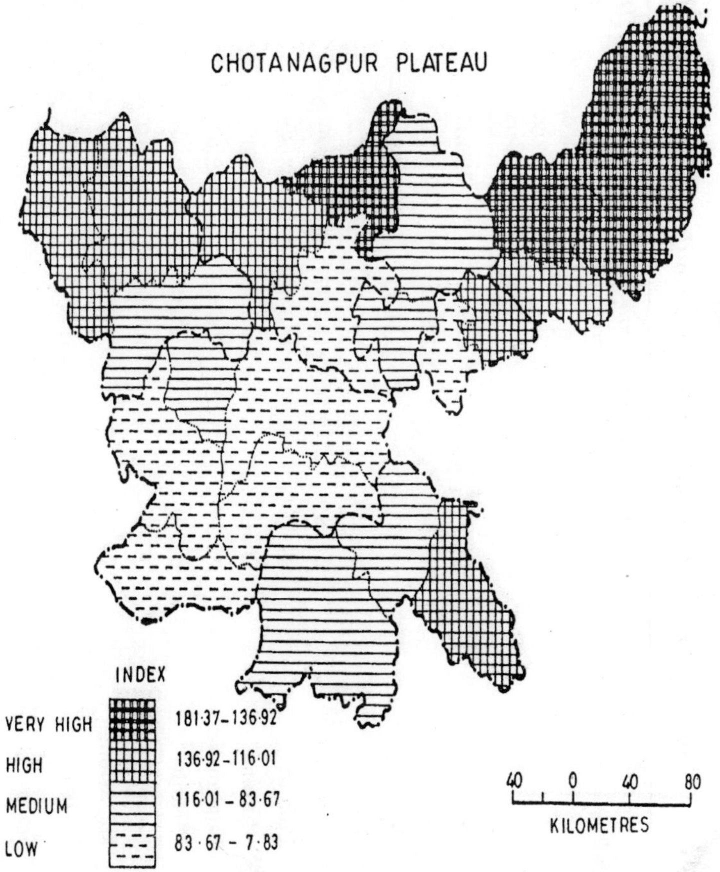

Figure 10

Disparities between Tribals and Non-tribals (Urban Population)

Table 16

Socio-economic Disparities between Tribals and Non-tribals (District-wise)

Subdivisions	*Literacy Differential*	*Urban Differential*	*Differential in Terms of Non-ag. Workers*	*Differential in Terms of Non-workers*	*Differential in Terms of Houseless*
–					
1. Dumka	35.95	159.92	62.21	63.31	136.84
2. Jamtara	5.43	121.25	8.01	125.19	119.15
3. Deoghar	43.24	141.71	54.21	146.96	161.19
4. Godda	121.35	141.18	75.82	109.19	180.95
5. Rajmahal	69. 99	183.37	69.99	93. 92	60.87
6. Pakaur	41.73	145.09	63.82	58.82	30.19
7. Dhanbad	106.42	123.10	56.17	163.31	89.26
8. Baghmara	69.14	7.83	152.05	171.88	73.87
9. Giridih	84.49	99.09	63 .18	162.09	110.87
10. Bermo	100.00	100.00	110.10	138.73	67.83
11. Hazaribagh	71.21	38.10	45.09	151.13	34.17
12. Chatra	47.74	119.86	36.96	184.00	39.37

(Contd...)

13.	Kodarma	75.68	180.45	32.52	194.50	75.09
14.	Daltonganj	58.25	132.67	63.13	167.82	113.86
15.	Latehar	6.26	83.72	53.78	73.43	68.46
16.	Garhwa	58.81	122.64	61.08	144.40	108.18
17.	Ranchi	51.07	57.78	51.07	86.58	102.87
18.	Khunti	14.63	82.18	43.65	45.02	144.15
19.	Simdega	0.86	41.64	35.29	2 8.84	182.69
20.	Gumla	9.04	83.60	46.85	31.59	63.44
21.	Lohardaga	36.70	114.72	53.66	52.07	76.31
22.	Chaibasa	36.12	93.04	71.86	36.69	85.89
23.	Seraikela	54.66	102.49	42.52	85.53	30.97
24.	Dalbhum	77.44	117.31	64.75	107.73	43.33

(Contd...)

Figure 10 shows regional pattern of inequality between tribals and non-tribals living in urban areas of Chotanagpur plateau. A cursory glance of the map indicates that urban differentials between tribal and non-tribal population are very high in the north-eastern part of the Chotanagpur plateau. This region consists of Rajmahal, Godda, Pakaur, Deoghar and Dumka. The Kodarma subdivision also comes under the category of very high urban differentials but found isolated from the main region.

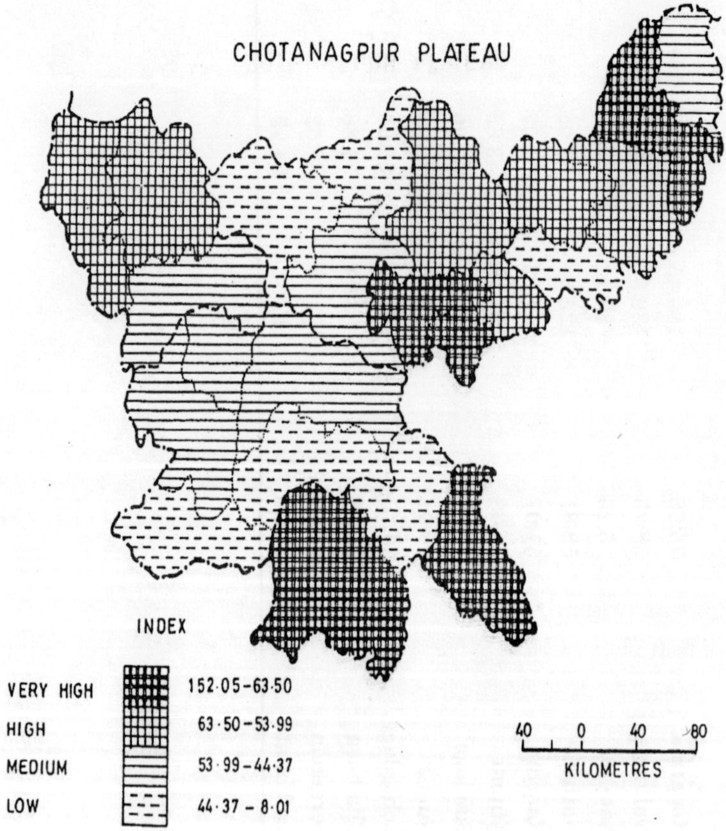

Figure 11

Disparities between Tribals and Non-tribals (Non-Agricultural Workers)

Three distinct regions of high urban differentials can be seen. One lies in the extreme north-west comprising Garhwa, Daltonganj and Chatra. The other two regions are located in the eastern and southern part representing Dhanbad, Jamtara and Dalbhum.

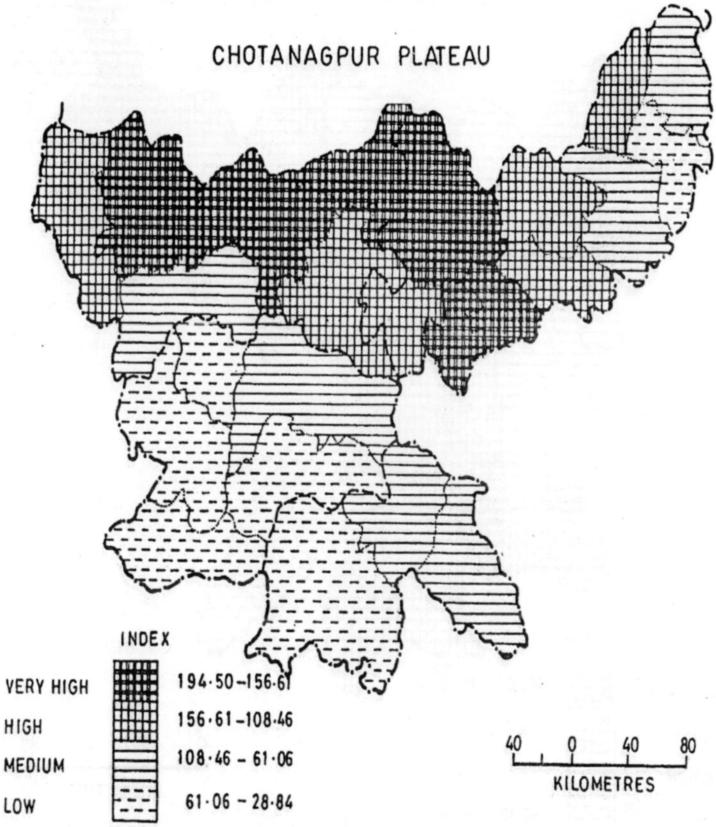

Figure 12

Disparities between Tribals and Non-tribals (Non-workers)

The regions of medium urban differentials are scattered in the western, southern and central part which consists of Latehar, Lohardaga, Seraikela, Chaibasa, Giridih and Bermo.

There is a very large compact region of low urban differentials located in central and eastern part which includes Baghmara, Hazaribagh, Ranchi, Khunti, Gumla and Simdega.

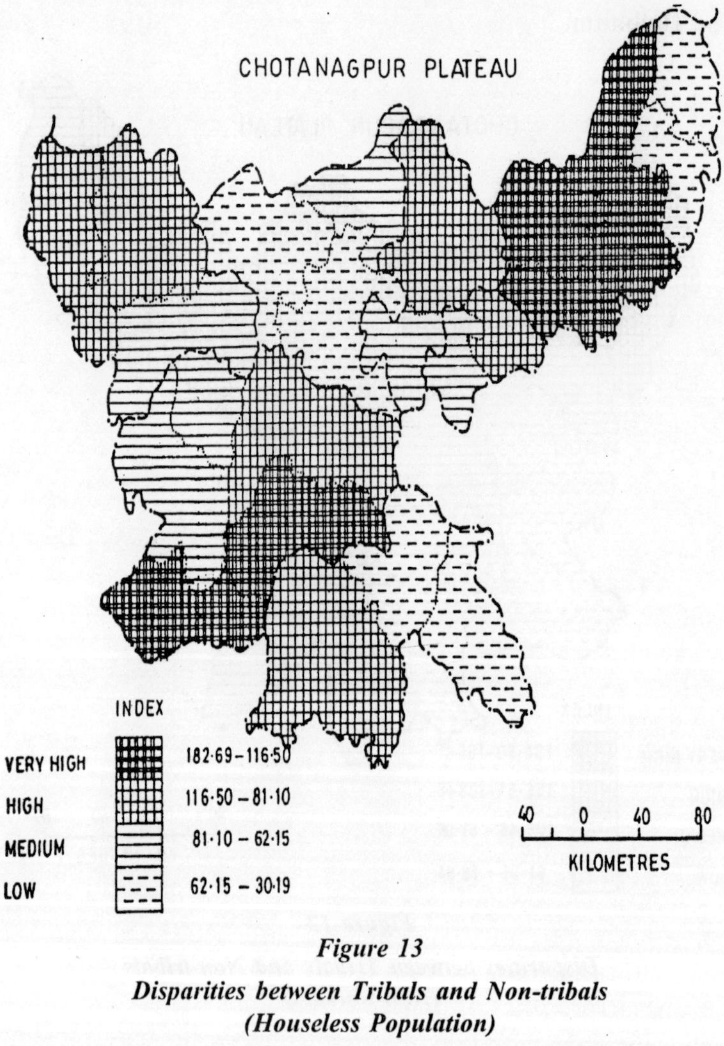

Figure 13

Disparities between Tribals and Non-tribals (Houseless Population)

The regional pattern of inequality in terms of non-agricultural workers between tribal and non-tribal population of

Chotanagpur plateau has been portrayed in Figure 11. It is revealed in the map that Godda, Pakaur Bermo, Baghmara, Dalbhum and Chaibasa record very high inequality which form three isolated regions located in the eastern, south-eastern and southern part of the study area.

The inequality in terms of non-agricultural workers among tribals and non-tribals is high in Garhwa, Daltonganj, Giridih, Dhanbad, Deoghar and Dumka.

There is a very large region of medium inequality located in the central-western part comprising Latehar, Lohardaga, Gumla, Simdega and Ranchi. Medium inequality in terms of non-agricultural workers may also be observed in Rajmahal subdivision which is located in the extreme north-eastern part of Chotanagpur.

The subdivision recording low inequality are Chatra, Kodarma, Simdega, Khunti, Seraikela and Jamtara.

The spatial pattern of inequality pertaining to non-workers between tribal and non-tribal population of Chotanagpur plateau is depicted in Figure 12. It may be noticed that the inequality is very high in Daltonganj, Chatra, Kodarma, Giridih, Dhanbad, and Baghmara subdivisions.

High inequality in terms of non-workers is found in Garhwa, Hazaribagh, Bermo, Deoghar, Godda and Jamtara.

The subdivisions recording medium inequality are Latehar, Ranchi, Seraikela, Dalbhum, Rajmahal and Dumka.

The area of low inequality comprises Lohardaga, Gumla, Simdega, Khunti, Chaibasa, and Pakaur.

Figure 13 shows spatial pattern of inequality as regards houselessness between the tribal and non-tribal population of Chotanagpur plateau. The inequality in terms of houselessness is very high in two regions which are located in the north-eastern and south-western parts. They includes: Godda, Deoghar, Dumka, Jamtara, Khunti and Simdega subdivisions.

The subdivisions which register high inequality in terms of houselessness are Garhwa, Daltonganj, Ranchi, Chaibasa Dhanbad and Giridih.

Medium inequality is observed in Latehar, Lohardaga, Gumla, Kodarma, Bermo and Baghmara.

Low inequality is found in Chatra, Hazaribagh, Seraikela, Dalbhum, Rajmahal and Pakaur.

7

Conclusion and Suggestions

The foregoing study shows that there are marked regional imbalances in the level of socio-economic development of Chotanagpur plateau (Jharkhand). The highly developed areas are small in extent and are largely confined to the south-eastern part, while the remaining parts are extremely backward. The developed areas comprise the subdivisions of Dhanbad, Baghmara, Ranchi, Chaibasa and Dalbhum. Their high level of socio-economic development may largely be attributed to their higher degree of industrialisation and urbanisation. The important industrial complex such as Sindri, Jharia, Bokaro, Patratu, Jamshedpur and Ranchi lie in these areas which have developed due to the advantage of being located in one of the richest mineral belts of the world. There is also good accessibility of railways and roads. Power network is also quite dense along with high potentiality for hydel and thermal power.

On the other hand, the underdevelopment of a large area of the north-western part of the Chotanagpur is on account of rugged forested topography, less developed means of communication and negligence of the government to develop this area. Thus, there are few islands of developed area in the vast ocean of underdevelopment. It is also revealed in the pattern of development that the industrialisation and urbanisation in some of the areas of Chotanagpur have very less degree of spread effect. This has increased the gap in the level of development between south-eastern and north-western Chotanagpur. It is desirable that in north-western Chotanagpur where conditions are not favourable for agriculture due to drought, rugged terrain and poor soil condition and also no big industrial establishment can be located. In the absence of infrastructure, small ancillary industries and forest-based industries should be encouraged. Thus in due course north-western Chotanagpur may succeed in having all suitable infrastructure for large industries. This may bring about some equity in the level of development and a better functional integration of industrial centres can be achieved.

The factorial analysis of the regional disparities in the study area has shown five dimensions which have been termed as : (i) Urbanisation and socio-economic development (ii) Institutional factors and agricultural development (iii) Work participation and infrastructural stress (iv) Educational status and (v) Miscellaneous factors.

The first factor urbanisation and socio-economic development accounts for 25.94 per cent of the total variance. The nature of the factor loadings indicates that almost all factors of socio-economic development are positively associated with urbanisation. The indicators which have very high positive loadings with urbanisation are the percentage of non-agricultural workers to the total population, percentage of pucca houses to the total houses, beds per lakh of population, doctors per lakh of population, number of police per lakh of population and number of registered working factories per 10,000 of population. This factor shows that there is concentration of amenities and facilities in urban centres and they are socially and economically more forward than their rural counterpart.

The spatial pattern of the first factor reveals that the areas of very high scores of socio-economic development comprise the subdivisions of Dhanbad, Baghmara and Ranchi. On the other hand, Deoghar, Jamtara, Dumka, Godda, Pakaur, Chatra, Latehar, Garhwa and Gumla subdivisions are very backward interms of socio-economic development.

The second dimension—institutional factor and agriculture development—explains 14.17 per cent of the total variance. It indicates that the size of land holdings has direct bearing on productivity. It has been observed that productivity of small and marginal farmers is moderate. Its reason is that most of the marginal and small farmers are poor and cannot afford to use modern agricultural inputs in their fields. Therefore, in spite of working hard in their field from dusk to dawn, they get poor yield. It is desired that for higher agricultural productivity the size of land holdings should neither be very small nor very big but medium. The medium farmers can easily afford the cost of modern inputs and also the medium size of holdings is managable.

The third factor is labelled as dimension of work participation and infrastructural stress. It accounts for 13.42 per cent of the total variance. The relationships of these factors reflect that this dimension has rural character. The percentage of main workers is comparatively higher in rural areas than urban centres because most of the family members in rural areas are engaged in primary activities, However, in terms of medical and educational facilities these areas have been neglected. Therefore, these areas must be given priority in opening new schools and hospitals on the basis of population concentration to be served.

It may be observed that the subdivisions recording high factor scores for work participation and infrastructural stress are Rajmahal, Godda, Pakaur, Deoghar, Dumka, Ranchi. Gumla, Simdega, Khunti and Seraikela. On the other hand,

Garhwa, Daltonganj, Kodarma, Hazaribagh, Bermo, Baghmara record low factor score while Chatra and Latehar very low factor scores of this dimension.

The fourth factor has been identified as educational status which explains 12.55 per cent of the total variance. It shows that in spite of concentration of schools in some part of the study area majority of its population remains illiterate and uneducated. It is due to the fact that tribals form a major proportion of the total population of Chotanagpur and owing to poverty and ignorance are still relevant towards formal education.

No doubt there has been some progress in education of scheduled tribes in Chotanagpur since independence, still there are a number of measures which should be undertaken to accelerate the pace of their educational development. At the pre-matric stage it is necessary not only to bring about larger enrolment but also to retain them in school. A great emphasis should be given on the quality of education. School facilities should be improved and expanded in remote areas. Teaching in the initial stage should be in the mother tongue of the students and the regional language should be introduced gradually to open the door to higher education. Greater care should be exercised in the recruitment and placement of the teachers in schools in the tribal areas so that not only are they conversant with the tribal language and culture but are also able to adapt themselves to the social, economic and physical environment. The school curriculums and programmes should be consistent with the situation in tribal areas. To the extent resources permit, single-teacher schools should give way to appointment of more than one teacher.

It is revealed that the subdivisions recording very high factor scores for educational status included Dhanbad, Baghmara, Ranchi, and Dalbhum while low factor scores for this dimension was observed in Dumka, Jamtara, Deoghar,

Chatra, Daltonganj, Latehar, Garhwa, Khunti, Simdega and Gumla.

The fifth factor is very diversified in nature which accounts for 11.71 per cent of the total variance. It shows that in Chotanagpur literacy is positively associated with net sown area. The very high scores for this dimension were recorded in Jamtara and Bermo subdivisions while there was very low score in the Latehar subdivision.

In the present study it has been observed that there is a wide gap in the socio-economic conditions of tribals and non-tribals in Chotanagpur plateau. The tribals are lagging far behind in almost all indicators of development such as literacy, non-agricultural workers, urban population, non-workers and housing. Table 15 shows that the percentage of tribal literates is 17.52 while it is 26.72 per cent in the case of non-tribals. The percentage of tribals engaged in non-agricultural activities is 5.18 per cent as against 9:80 per cent of non-tribals. Similarly, the percentage of tribal houseless population and people living in urban areas are 9.80 per cent and 5.18 per cent respectively whereas these figures are 2.83 per cent and 26.35 per cent among non-tribals. One interesting finding which has emerged is that the percentage of tribal non-workers is lower than the non-tribals. The percentage of non-workers among the tribals is 15.10 per cent whereas it is 62.73 per cent among non-tribals.

In the light of the above discussion it may be concluded that the tribes of Chotanagpur have not benefited to the desired extent by its modern industrialisation programmes. They had to lose their means of subsistence for mining and establishment of industrial complexes which made them unemployed. Then they could not get jobs substantially in the industries due to lack of requisite training and skill. This led to the sharp gap in employment and resultant prosperity between masses of poor tribals and microscopic elite tribals and majority of non-tribals.

The ability to face the harsh forces of the modern industrial age has to be built into the tribals through education. Skills should be imparted in advance to enable the tribal communities to avail industrial opportunities in the new establishment. If not the first generation, individuals belonging to the second generation might absorb the skills. Traditional tribal handicrafts and products of arts should be encouraged. Forest-based cottage and small scale industries should be encouraged.

One can put forward the argument that the spatial distribution of disparity is the result of spatially segregated functions within the economic system. In the logical scheme of things, in the broad context, some regions, because of natural and historical reasons, are more developed than the others leading to marked variations in the 'socio-economic landscape'. The allocative mechanism involved in the spatial distribution of developmental resources invariably operates in favour of the developed regions with the result that the economic rewards accruing to different regions are unequal. This has led to spatially segregated quality of life. Once the process of cumulative causation creates regional disparities by favouring the more developed regions it is very difficult to reverse the trend because of the multiplier effect of greater economic development. Therefore, the region in which a person lives is a matter of great importance in terms of income, employment and the general quality of life in basically a laissez-faire system.

The basic drawback of these development schemes in the opinion of author was that the sub-plans were formulated on an ad hoc basis and the backward subdivisions were not identified on any scientific basis nor was their relative backwardness *vis-a-vis* other subdivisions clearly understood.

During the successive plans a growing concern for the backward regions was professed and it became the broad objective of the planning process to reduce the disparities in social services and economic infrastructure between the backward and developed areas but this laudable wish was not matched by any clear-cut formulation of specific objectives.

Even though the planning processes, both at the regional as well as the sectoral levels have stimulated considerable economic development in absolute terms, they have failed to eliminate or reduce regional disparities. The reasons lie both at the conceptual as well as at the implementation levels.

One feels that there is a perceptible lack of genuine moral commitment to the ideal of elimination of disparities because it goes against the vested interest of the ruling elite. Without social commitment and the requisite political will nothing of real significance is going to be achieved. The combination of social commitment and political will of implementation is not easy to achieve as it relates to contradiction. The combination calls for major structural changes in society. A policy positive discrimination in favour of the backward regions in terms of fiscal allocation, policy formulation and its implementation must be adopted. The logic behind the policy of statutory discrimination in favour of scheduled tribes and scheduled castes can be extended and made applicable to the undeprived regions as well. At the operation level this can be achieved through fiscal measures like allocation of plan outlays and by a system of incentives aimed at attracting private capital to backward regions. This is not to suggest that the developed regions should be denied their legitimate share, but that it is absolutely necessary to accelerate the rate of investment in backward regions if disparities both in absolute and relative terms are to be effectively minimised.

Fortunately, in the Indian federal structure, avenues for the flow of resources among states and regions exist, and given the political will the desired result can be achieved through a wide range of strategies:

i) direct investment by the government in backward regions.

ii) licensing policies and various incentives to attract private capital.

iii) investment policies favouring backward regions by financial institutions.

iv) meso and micro-level integrated planning should take into account the local resource, potential and the needs and aspirations of the common people.

Bibliography

Books

Ahmad, Q., *Indian Cities : Characteristics and Correlates,* research paper No. 102, The Dept. of Geography; University of Chicago, 1965.

Ahmed, E., *Bihar : A Physical Economic and Regional Geography,* Ranchi University, Ranchi, 1965.

Ahluwalia, M.S., *Income Inequality Some Dimension of the Problem,* Oxford Univ. Press, New Delhi, 1979.

Ahuja, K., *Idle Labour in Village India*, Manohar Pub., New Delhi, 1978.

Andrew, F.M., and Withy S.B., *Social Indicators of Well-being,* Plenum Press, New York, 1976.

Atkinson, A.B., *The Economics of Inequality*, Oxford Press, Clarendon, 1975.

Bhatt, A., *Caste, Class and Politics,* Concept Pub., New Delhi, 1975.

Beteille A., *The Idea of Natural Inequality and Other Essays,* Oxford University Press, Bombay, 1983.

Bose, S.R. and Shosh. P.P., *Agro-economic Survey of Bihar: A Pilot Study*, B.K. Publishers, Patna, 1976.

Bourne, L.S., *The Geography of Housing,* Edward Arnold Publishers Ltd., London, 1981.

Chandhary, B. (ed.) *Tribal Development in India: Problems and Prospects,* Inter India publications, Delhi, 1981.

Chishlom, M., et al. (ed.), *Regional Forecasting*, Butterworth, London, 1971.

Coates, B.E., et al., *Geography and Inequality*, Oxford Press, 1977.

Das, K.N., *Essays in Geography*, Department of Geography, Bhagalpur University, Bhagalpur. 1969.

Desai, P.B., *Planning in India, 1951-1978,* New Delhi: Vikas Pub., House, 1979.

Dube, S.C., *Development Perspectives for the 1980's,* Abhinav Publications, New Delhi, 1983.

Ganguli, B.N. (ed.), *Concept of Equality: The Nineteenth Century Indian Debate*, Indian Institute of Advanced Study, Simla, 1975.

Gupta, B.D., Urbanisation in Bengal and Changing rural-urban interaction patterns, Chaudhary M.K. (ed.), *Trends in Socio-economic Change in India:1871-1961*, IIAS, Simla, 1969,

Gupta, P.S., and Sdayuk, G., "Economic Regionalisation of India-Problems and Approaches", *Census of India 1961. Monograph Series*, Vol, I, No. 8

Harvey, D., *Social Justice and the City,* London : Edward Arnold, 1973.

Hirschman, A.O., *The Strategy of Economic Development,* Yale Univ. Press, Connecticut, 1958.

Hoselitz, B.F., and Moore, W.E., *Industrialization and Society,* UNESCO, Moulton, 1970.

Hoyle, B.S., *Spatial Aspects of Development,* John Wiley & Sons Ltd, 1978.

ICCSR, CSO, *Social Information of India: Trends and Structure,* Hindustan Publishing Corporation, New Delhi, 1983.

Isard, W., et al., *General Theory: Social Economic and Regional*, MIT Press, Cambridge, 1969.

Johnston, J.N., *Indicators of Education System,* UNESCO, International Institute of Educational Planning, 1981.

Johnston, R.J., *Multivariate Statistical Analysis in Geography,* Longman Pub., London, 1978.

King, M., (ed.) *Medical Care in Developing Countries,* Oxford Univ. Press, Nairobi, 1966.

Knox, P.L., *Social Well-being: A Spatial Perspective,* Oxford University Press, 1975.

Kulkarni, K.M., *Geography of Crowding and Human Response,* Concept Publishing Company, New Delhi, 1984.

Kundu, A., and Raza, M., *Indian Economy: The Regional Dimension,* Centre for the Study of Regional Development, J.N,U., New Delhi, 1982,

Kurien, C.T., *Poverty Planning and Social Transformation Alternatives in Development Planning,* New Delhi, ICSSR, 1978.

Kuznets, S., *Modern Economic Growth: Rate Structure and Spread,* Yale Univ. Press, Connecticut, 1966.

___________, Consumption, Industrialisation and Urbanisation in Hoselitz, B. F. (eds.) *Industrialisation and Society,* UNESCO: Moulton, 1970.

Mahajan, V.S., *Planning and Socialistic Transformation of Indian Economy,* Deep and Deep Pub. New Delhi, 1982.

Mahmood, A., *Statistical Methods in Geographical Studies,* Rajesh Pub. New Delhi, 1977.

Majumdar, D.N., *Races and Cultures of India,* Asia Publishing House, Bombay, 1981.

Majumdar, P.S., and Majumdar, I., *Rural Migrants in an Urban Setting,* Hindustan Pub. Co., New Delhi, 1978.

Marks, K., *Wage Labour and Capital,* New York, International Publishers, 1933,

Misra, R.P., *Contribution to Indian Geography in Regional Development,* Heritage Publishers, New Delhi, 1988.

__________, et al. *Regional Planning in India, A Strategy Institute,* Mysore Instt. of Development Studies, 1974.

Mitra, A., and Mukharji, S., *Population, Food and Land Inequality in India, 1971, A Geography of Hunger and Insecurity,* Allied Pub., 1980

Mohammad, N., *Caste and Primary Occupations, A Geographical Analysis,* Concept Publishing Company, New Delhi,1987.

Mukherjee, A,B., *The Chamars of Uttar Pradesh: A Study in Social Geography,* Inter Indian Publications, Delhi, 1979.

Myrdal, G.M., *Economic Theory and Under Development,* Duckworth Pub. London, 1957.

Nair, K.R,G. (ed.), *Regional Disparities in India,* Agricole Publishing (academy, New Delhi, 1981.

Najundappa, D.M., and Sinha R.K., *Backward Area Development: Problems and Prospects,* Sterling Publishers Private Limited, New Delhi, 1982.

Noble, A.G., et al., *Indian Urbanisation and Planning: Vehicles of Modernisation,* Tata McGraw Hill Publishing Company Ltd., New Delhi, 1977.

Oberai, A.S., and Singh H.K.M., *Causes and Consequences of Internal Migration,* Oxford University Press, New Delhi, 1983.

Pandit, S.N., *Critical Study of Agricultural Productivity in Uttar Pradesh—1951-75,* Concept Pub. Company, New Delhi, 1982.

Pandey, R., *Social Inequality; Features Forms and Functions,* Anju Publishers, Lucknow, 1982.

Pigou, A.C., *The Economics of Welfare,* MacMilan Pub., London, 1920.

Pranjpe, A.C., *Caste Prejudice and the Individual,* Lavani Publishing House, 1970.

Punit, A.B., *Profiles of Poverty in India,* B.R. Publishing Corporation, Delhi,1982.

Rao, D.V.R., *Dimensions of Backwardness*, Concept Publishing Company, New Delhi, 1981.

Rao, H., *Regional Disparities and Development in India*, Ashish Publishing House, New Delhi,1984.

Rao, M.V.S., et al., *Indicators of Human and Social Development,* United Nations, University Press, 1978.

Sachchidanda and Mardal B.B., *Industrialisation and Social Disorganisation,* Concept Publishing Company, New Delhi, 1984.

Seligman, E.R.A., and Johnson, A., *Encyclopedia of Social Sciences*, Vol. 13-14, Macmillan, 1957.

Sengupta, Syamlakanli, *Caste Status, Group Aggregate and Class,* Firma KLM Private Limited, Calcutta, 1979,

Shafi, M., *Agricultural Productivity and Regional Imbalances A Study of Uttar Pradesh,* Concept Pub. Co., New Delhi, 1984.

__________ and Aziz. A. (ed.), *Food Systems of the World,* Rawat Publications, Jaipur, 1989.

Sharma, R.C., *Regional Planning for Social Development,* Criterion Publications, New Delhi, .1989,

Sharma, S.K., and Malhotra, S.L., *Integrated Rural Development,* Abhinav Publications, New Delhi, 1977.

Sinclair, H.M., *Nutrition and Health*, Faber and Faber Ltd., London, 1961.

Singh, C., *India's Poverty and Its Solution*, Bombay; Asia Pub. House, 1964.

Singh, H.P., *Resource Appraisal and Planning in India,* Rajesh Publications, New Delhi, 1979.

Singh, A.K., *Patterns of Regional Development—A Comparative Study*, Sterling Pub. New Delhi, 1981.

Singh, K.S., (ed,), *Economics of the Tribes and Their Transformation,* Concept Publishing Company, New Delhi, 1982.

Singh., Hanuman (ed.), *Planning Regional Development and Disparities in India*, Criterion Publications, 1989.

Sinha, V.C. and Zacharia, E., *Elements of Demography,* Allied Publishers Private Ltd, 1982.

Smith, D.M., *The Geography of Social Well-being in the United States*, MacGraw Hill, New York, 1973.

__________, *Human Geography: A Welfare Approach*, Edward Arnold, London, 1977.

__________, *Where the Grass is Greener: Living in an Unequal World,* Penguin, London, 1979.

Srinivasan, T.N., and Bardhan, P.K. (eds.), *Poverty and Income Distribution*, Calcutta, Statistical Pub. Society, 1974.

Sundram, K.V., *Geography of Under Development*, Concept Publishing Company, New Delhi, 1983.

Teresa, H., *The Creation of World Poverty*, Selected Book Service Publication, New Delhi, 1982.

Tewari, R.T., *Changing Patterns of Development in India*, Ashish Publishing House, New Delhi, 1984.

Tilak, T.B., *Educational and Regional Development*, Yatna Publications, New Delhi, 1986.

Torstan, H., (ed.), *The International Encyclopides of Education*, Pergamon Press, 1985.

UNESCO, The Use of Socio-economic Indicators in Development Planning.

Wilcox, C., *Towards Social Welfare*, Richard, D. Irwin Pub., Homewood, 1969.

Wilson, J., *Equality*, Hutchinson Press, London, 1966.

Journals

Abram, M., "Subjective social Indicators", *Social Trends*, Vol. 4, pp. 3 5-50, 1973.

Hndrew, M., "Geography and the Study of Human Well-being", *Geographical Viewpoint*, Vol. 7, pp. 45-55, 1978,

__________, "Area Based Positive Discrimination and the Distribution of well-being", *Institute of British Geographers*, Vol. 6. No. 1, pp. 53-67, 1981.

Banerji, D., "Health Behaviour of Rural populations Impact of Rural Health Services", *Economic and Political Weekly*, 8, pp. 2264, and 2267, 1973.

Bahadur, S., and Ahmed, A., "Inequalities in Higher Education in India", *Indian Journal of Regional Science*, Vo1.8, No. 2, pp. 12-20, 1981.

Berry, B.J.L., "More on Relevance and policy Analysis", *Area*, Vol. 5, No. 2, pp. 158-59, 1972.

Bhat, L.S., "Problems of Regionalisation for the Development of National Economy", *Sankhya*, Series B. Vol. 25, pp. 5-14.

Bronger, D., "Regional Disparities as a Problem of Spatial Development Planning in Countries of Third World: Case of India with Reference to Andhra Pradesh", *Annals of the National Association of Geographers India*, Vol, 6, No. 1, pp. 14-35, 1986.

Burke, F., "Spatial Disparities in the Literacy of Scheduled Castes of Uttar Pradesh, *Geographical Review*, Vo1. 46, No.4 pp. 88-97, Dec. 1984.

Bodermann, Y.M, et al., "The Micro Organisation of Backwardness in Central Saridinia: A Reappraisal of Luxemberg's Three Phases of Under Development", *Journal of Peasant Studies*, Vol.7, No. 4, pp. 458-76, 1980.

Chattopadhya, B. and Raza, M., "Regional Development: Analytical Framework and Indicators", *Journal of Regional Science*, Vol. 7, No. 1, pp. 45-52, 1975.

Clark, G.L., "Capitalism-and Regional Inequality", *Annals of the Association of American Geographers*, Vo1.70, No. 2, pp. 226-37, 1980.

Dadibhavi, R.V., "An Analysis of Inter-Taluk Disparity and Backwardness in Karnataka State", *Indian Journal of Regional Science*, Vol, 14, No.2, pp. 166-173,1982.

Dale, B., "Subjective and Objective Social Indicators in Studies of Regional Social Well-being", *Regional Studies*, Vol. 14, No. 6, pp. 503-15, 1980.

Duncan, S., "The Plight of African", *Tropical Talks*, Vol, 23, 1970.

Lcholes, J.M., "Trends in Social Expenditure Inequality across Soviet Republics: A Comment", *Soviet Studies*, Vol. 32, No 3, pp. 428-30, 1980.

Ernest, M., "Marxist Economic Theory", *Monthly Review Press*, Vol. 1, pp. 155, New York, 1970.

Eyles, J., "Geography and Relevance", *Area*, Vo1.5. No. 2, pp.158-59, 1973.

Fair, T.J.D., "Population", *South African Geographical Journal*, Vol. 52, pp. 69-71, 1970.

Gradus, Y.Y., "The Role of Politics in Regional Inequality: The Israeli Case", *Annals of the Association of American Geographers*, Vol. 73, No.3, pp. 388-40, 1983.

Gulati, S.C., "Dimension of Inter-District Disparities", *Indian Journal of Regional Science*, Vol. No.1, pp. 69-71, 1977.

Hansen, F., "Regional Growth and Regional Problems, *Capitalism Geografisk Tidscrift*, Vol. 8, pp. 109-13, 1980.

Helbrun, N., "Geography and the Quality of Life", *Annals of the Association of American Geographers*, Vol. 72, No. 4, pp.445-55, 1982.

Jhonston, R.J., "But some are more equal, Who gets What where and How", *New Zealand Geographers*, Vol. 60, No. 4, pp. 255-268, 1976.

Kearsly, G.W., "Subjective Social Indicators and the Quality of Life in Dunedin", *New Zealand Geographers*, Vol. 38, No. 1, pp. 19-24, 1982.

Knox, P.L., "Level of Living : A Conceptual Framework For Monitoring Regional Variation in Well-being", *Regional Studies*, Vol. 8, No. 13, pp. 11-18, 1974.

Knox, P.L., and Cottam M.B., "A Welfare Approach to Rural Geography: Contrasting Perspective on the Quality of Higland's Life", *Institute of British Geographers*, Vol.6.

Loronz, M.O., "Methods of Measuring the Concentration of Wealth", *The Quarterly Publication of the American Statistical Association*, Vol. 9, No. 7, pp. 209-19, 1905

Majumdar, M., "Regional Disparities in India", *Urban Studies,* pp. 343-349, 1978.

McGrahan, D., "Development Indicators and Development", *Journal of Development Studies*, Vol, 8, 1972.

Mishra, K. and Gaikerad, S.B., "Impacts of Economic Development on Welfare and Living Conditions of People of M.P", *Indian Journal of Regional Science*, Vol. 11, No. 1, pp. 25-35, 1970.

Nair, K,R.G., "Regional Disparities in Industrial Wages", *Indian Journal of Regional Science*, Vol. 9, No. 2, 1977.

Nechernis, C., "Regional Differentiation of Living Standards in the R.S.F.R.: The Issue of Inequality", *Soviet Studies*, Vol. 23, No. 3, pp. 366-78, 1980.

Peet, R., "Inequality and Poverty: A Marxist-Geographic Theory", *Annals of the Association of American Geographers*, Vol. 65, into. 4, pp. 564-72, 1975.

Prakash, S., "Regional Inequalities and Economic Development with Special Reference to Infrastructural Facilities", *Indian Journal of Regional Science*, Vol. 9, No.2, pp. 172-194, 1977.

___________,and Rajan, P., "Regional Inequalities in Madhya Pradesh", *Indian Journal of Regional Science*, Vo1.11, No. 1, pp. 1-12, 1979.

Ramna. K. V. and Sharma, R. V., "Disparities in Development: A. Block Level Study of Telangana Region", *Indian Journal of Regional Science*, Vol. 11, No. 1, pp. 55-67 1979.

Sampath, R.K., "Inter-state Inequalities in Income in India", *Indian Journal of Regional Science*, Vol. 9,1977.

Saur, D., "Development Indicators in Identification and Regional Disparity, in Orissa: A Factor Analytic Study", *Indian Journal of Regional Science*, Vol. 16, No. 2, pp. 10 8-20, 1984.

Sharma, P.N., "Regional Planning—A case study of Uttar Pradesh", *Eastern Economist*, Vol, 60, No. 5, pp. 108-89, 1972.

___________, and Katiyar, P.C., "Identifying underdeveloped District of Uttar Pradesh", *Indian Journal of Regional Science*, Vol. 6, No. 1, pp. 30-38, 1974.

Siddiqi, A.H., 'Regional Inequality in the Development of Pakistan", *Geo-Journal*, Vol. 5, No. 1, pp. 17-32, 1980.

Singh, A.K., "Regional Inequalities in A Backward Economy: A Study of Trends in Inter-Regional and Inter-District Income Disparities in Uttar Pradesh", *Indian Journal of Regional Science*, Vol. 11, No. 1, pp. 36-47, 1979.

Smith, D.M., "Alternative 'Relevant' Professional Role", *Area*, Vol. 5, No. 1, pp. 1-4, 1973.

__________,"WHO gets WHAT WHERE and HOW: A Welfare Focus for Human Geography", *Geography*, Vol, 59, No. 264, pp. 289-97, 1974.

__________, "On the concept of Welfare", *Area,* Vol. 7, No.l, pp, 33-36, 1975.

Tam, M.V.S., and Persky, J., "Regional Convergence and Inequality", *Perksy Review of Economics and Statistics*, Vol. 67. No. 1, pp. 161-65, 1981.

Varma, P.C., "Regional Disparity in Per capita Product in Pakistan", *Indian Journal of Regional Science*, Vo1.4, No. 1, PP, 90-98, 1972.

Williamson, A,G., "An Analysis of South African", *Bulletin of Conference Socialist Economics*, Vol. 4, No.1, pp.1-38, 1965.

Bulletins and Reports

Statistical Handbook of Bihar, 1982, Directorate of Statistics and Evaluation. Govt. of Bihar.

Bihar: Through Figures, 1981, Directorate of Statistics and Evaluation, Government of Bihar.

Land and People of Tribal Bihar, Bihar Tribal Research Institute, 1961.

Report on Agricultural-Census 1970-71, Bihar, Government of Bihar.

Census of India, 1981, Series-4, Bihar, Special Tables for Scheduled Tribes, part IX (IV).

__________, Series-4, Bihar, Special Tables for Scheduled Tribes, part IX (III).

__________, Series-4. Bihar, Primary Census abstract of Scheduled Castes and Scheduled Tribes, part II of 1982.

__________, Series-4. Bihar, General Population Tables, part II-A.

__________, Series -4, Bihar, Census Atlas, part XII.

District census Hand books Village and Town Directory of Santhal Pargana, Singhbhum, Hazaribagh, Giridih, Palamau, Ranchi and Dhanbad, part XIII-A.

Index